Infinite Hope

A Black Artist's Journey from World War II to Peace

Ashley Bryan

A Caitlyn Dlouhy Book

ATHENEUM BOOKS FOR YOUNG READERS

New York London Toronto Sydney New Delhi

**To my dear editor, Caitlyn (Meis) Dlouhy,
and in acknowledgment of the 502nd Port Battalion
of stevedore soldiers**

Ⓐ atheneum ATHENEUM BOOKS FOR YOUNG READERS • An imprint of Simon & Schuster Children's Publishing Division • 1230 Avenue of the Americas, New York, New York 10020 • Text copyright © 2019 by The Ashley Bryan Center, a Maine Corporation • This work is a memoir. It reflects the author's present recollections of his experiences over a period of years. • All rights reserved, including the right of reproduction in whole or in part in any form. • ATHENEUM BOOKS FOR YOUNG READERS is a registered trademark of Simon & Schuster, Inc. Atheneum logo is a trademark of Simon & Schuster, Inc. • For information about special discounts for bulk purchases, please contact Simon & Schuster Special Sales at 1-866-506-1949 or business@simonandschuster.com. • The Simon & Schuster Speakers Bureau can bring authors to your live event. For more information or to book an event, contact the Simon & Schuster Speakers Bureau at 1-866-248-3049 or visit our website at www.simonspeakers.com. • Book design by Irene Metaxatos • The text for this book was set in Bookman Old Style. • Manufactured in China • 0719 SCP • First Edition • 10 9 8 7 6 5 4 3 2 1 • Library of Congress Cataloging-in-Publication Data • Names: Bryan, Ashley, author, illustrator. • Title: Infinite hope : a black artist's journey from World War II to peace / Ashley Bryan. • Description: First edition. | New York : Atheneum Books for Young Readers, [2019] | Audience: Ages 10 up. | Audience: Grades 4 to 6. | "A Caitlyn Dlouhy Book." • Identifiers: LCCN 2019015826 | ISBN 9781534404908 (hardback) | ISBN 9781534404915 (eBook) • Subjects: LCSH: Bryan, Ashley. | Illustrators—United States—Biography—Juvenile literature. | African American illustrators—Biography—Juvenile literature. | Soldiers—United States—Biography—Juvenile literature. | African American soldiers—Biography—Juvenile literature. | World War, 1939–1945—Participation, African-American—Juvenile literature. | BISAC: JUVENILE NONFICTION / History / Military & Wars. | JUVENILE NONFICTION / Biography & Autobiography / Historical. | JUVENILE NONFICTION / People & Places / United States / African American. • Classification: LCC NC975.5.B79 A2 2019 | DDC 741.6092 [B]—dc23 • LC record available at https://lccn.loc.gov/2019015826 • Note on text: All of Ashley Bryan's letters and journal entries have been transcribed as written by him. Dates have been added wherever clarification was needed, and abridged for content or spacing where necessary.

CONTENTS

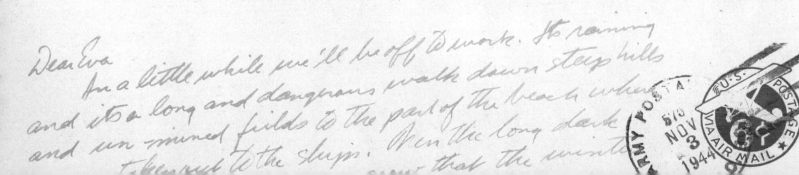

Dear Eva
In a little while we'll be off @ work. It's raining
and it's a long and dangerous walk down steep hills
and un mined fields to the part of the beach where
take out to the ships. Now the long dark
now that the winter

U. S. DECLARES STATE OF WAR

One Battleship Lost, 1,500 Killed in Hawaii

FDR Aide Bares Toll In Air Raid

Navy's Failure To Block Quick Blow Explained

WASHINGTON, Dec. 8 (UP).—The United States forces have destroyed "a number of Japanese planes and submarines" in operations against Japan in the battle of the Pacific, the White House announced today, and the Japanese dive bomber attacks on Hawaii left 3,000 casualties.

White House Secretary Stephen T. Early announced that 1,500 persons were wounded and about the same number killed in the dive bomber attacks which Japan launched on the island of Oahu at dawn yesterday. He added that despite the large number of bombs dropped upon the city of Honolulu itself, there were relatively few casualties there.

Asked how he deemed it possible for the Japanese aircraft to pierce the outer defenses of the United States' strongholds in the Pacific, Early gave this explanation as representing "expert consensus":

"Probably most if not all, of the planes that attacked came from Japanese carriers. The planes were the dive-bomber type. The attack came at dawn and the carriers naturally would have had all night, under cover of darkness, to approach."

Counter-Offensive Begins

Naval officials, meanwhile, said that the counter-offensive against Japan began the moment the first Japanese bomb exploded on the islands.

The White House statement said:

"American operations against the Japanese attacking force in the neighborhood of the Hawaiian islands are still continuing. A number of Japanese planes and submarines have been destroyed.

See FDR AIDE BARES
(Page 2 Column 4)

Lewis Victor in Mine Edict

NEW YORK, Dec. 8 (UP).— The United Mine Workers of America (CIO) last night won 2-to-1 arbitration board decision awarding a union shop in captive mines owned by the country's major steel producers. The decision was announced by John R. Steelman, chairman of the board who recently received leave of absence as director of U. S. conciliation service to act of the arbitrators.

John L. Lewis, president of the union, agreed with Steelman in a majority opinion. Benjamin Fairless, president of the United States Steel corporation.
See LEWIS VICTOR
(Page 2, Column 8)

Japanese Embassy Staff Burns Papers

Now We Know—and We Stand Firm

After the first cold, brutal shock, after the flaming resentment, born of surprise and pain, one can hear on all sides now: "Well, at last we know where we stand."

With the reports still coming in and still lacking confirmation of the sinking of this battleship and that, and the downing of so many planes and the quick, sudden death of men caught in their barracks, so much at least is certain—"At last, we know where we stand." Events not of this country's making, circumstances which were until now beyond its control, have thrust the United States into the world-wide war, and in that emergency the nation stands resolute and firm.

There will be no more of appeasement. The long and tiresome diplomatic conversations, the exchange of notes and the efforts at concealment are at an end. There will be no more of the long and trying debate concerning who or what was trying to inch this country into a war in which it had no genuine interest. Bombs on a distant island have drowned out that academic discourse. The war, as might have been expected, as wise men have freely predicted, has come to this country. There is no need to debate.

There is time only to declare war and then win it—as quickly and as crushingly as possible. It will not be an easy task. As always, the initial advantage lies with the aggressor.

Japanese embassy staff members put the match quickly to piles of papers, presumably important documents, after their nation attacked Hawaii and Guam. Scene of fire above is embassy's back lawn in Washington. Japanese

Ambassador Nomura is shown below as he glanced at his watch as zero hour in the Pacific crisis arrived. He and Emergency Envoy Kurusu are pictured at state department in Washington.

Great Naval Engagement Under Way in Mid-Ocean

HONOLULU, Dec. 8 (UP).— United States and Japanese fleets were believed fighting in mid-Pacific today after a Japanese aerial bombing attack on the Hawaiian islands opened war between the two great Pacific powers.

The American fleet steamed out...

Lone Vote Against War Cast Following President's Appeal

WASHINGTON, Dec. 8 (UP).—Congress today proclaimed existence of a state of war between the United States and the Japanese empire 33 minutes after the dramatic moment when President Roosevelt stood before a joint session to pledge that we will triumph—"so help us, God."

The senate acted first, adopting the resolution by a unanimous roll call vote of 82 to 0.

(See LONE VOTE AGAINST, Page 7, Column 1)

By Lyle C. Wilson
(Associated Press Correspondent)

WASHINGTON, Dec. 8 (UP).—President Roosevelt today in person asked congress to declare that "a state of war has existed between the United States and the Japanese empire" as a result of Japan's "unprovoked and dastardly attack."

The President made his request to a joint session of congress, giving it a brief but detailed account of Japan's attack on American territory yesterday—a date which he said "will live in infamy."

"The facts of yesterday speak for themselves," he said. "The people of the United States have already formed their opinions and will understand the implications to the very life and safety of our nation.

"As commander-in-chief of the army and navy, I have directed that all measures be taken for our defense.

"Always will we remember the character of the onslaught against us."

He predicted that the American people "in their righteous might

British Join U. S. in War

Churchill Cites Far East Attack

NEW YORK, Dec. 8 (UP).— The Rome radio said today in a broadcast that the Japanese declaration of war "involves, in accordance with the three-power pact, the existence of a state of war between the two Axis powers and the United States." CBS heard the broadcast.

CHUNGKING, Dec. 8 (UP).— Chinese Foreign Minister Quo Tai-chi today said China has decided... against... well... the... nev... tion...

Heavy Toll Claimed

TOKYO, Dec. 8 (UP).—The navy section of the imperial headquarters announced today two American battleships were sunk, four others damaged and four heavy cruisers damaged at Pearl Harbor by Japanese naval bombers during the attack yesterday.

The naval statement, broadcast on the Tokyo radio, said there were no Japanese losses. Imperial headquarters also declared that a United States aircraft carrier was sunk by a submarine off Honolulu.

It said Japanese planes which attacked Guam early today were reported without confirmation to have sunk the 810 sweeper Penguin...

-: Late War Bulletins :-

NEW YORK, Dec. 8 (UP).—The National Broadcasting company's correspondent at Manila reported today that "Manila is now under Japanese bombardment."

NEW YORK, Dec. 8 (UP).—Federal bureau of investigation agents and New York police at 6 a. m. today had rounded up 85 Japanese in New York City considered "dangerous" to the country's security. Most of them were taken to Ellis island, but some were detained for questioning.

NEW YORK, Dec. 8 (UP).—The German radio announced today that Manchukuo had declared war on the United States and Great Britain. NBC heard the broadcast.

NEW YORK, Dec. 8 (UP).—At least 290 casualties were reported today after two air raids on the Philippine islands by high-flying Japanese planes, Thomas Worthen, CBS correspondent in Manila, said today in a broadcast from that city.

ROME, Dec. 8 (UP).—The Rome radio today blamed hostilities in the Far East on President Roosevelt, saying "as a result of Roosevelt's war mongering program the first hostilities occurred between Japanese and American forces."

Nazis See 'World Curse' on FDR; U. S.-Reich Status 'Unimportant'

BERLIN, Dec. 8 (UP).—A Wilhelmstrasse spokesman said today the curse of the entire world would rest upon President Roosevelt, whom he called "the father of war," as he commented on the Far Eastern war.

He said he was not authorized to expound on the international angle as to who was the aggressor. However, he stated: "But from my commentary there should be little doubt about that."

As seen from a historical point of view, he asserted, it was unimportant whether war would be declared between Germany and the United States as a result of Far Eastern events.

LONDON, Dec. 8 (UP).—The Exchange Telegraph agency reported that 30 planes bombed Hong Kong this morning, causing slight damage.

LONDON, Dec. 8 (UP).—Reuters said in a dispatch from Singapore today that a British communique declared "it is unofficially reported but not confirmed that mustard gas has been "dropped" in Japanese attacks on Malaya.

LONDON, Dec. 8 (UP).—British authorities today began a roundup of Japanese nationals in the United Kingdom. Representatives of Domei, Japanese news agency, were among the first taken into custody.

TOKYO, Dec. 8 (UP).—Army and navy sections of the imperial headquarters announced today that 50 or 60 American planes were shot down in air combats over Clark field, in the Philippines and 40 more over Iba, 80 miles northeast of Manila. Domei broadcast the announcement.

TOKYO, Dec. 8 (UP).—The Japanese information bureau announced today that about 100 British and American other foreign nationals were... throughout the Japanese... nouncement...

A Victory mural. That was what I, along with other art students, was busy painting when the notice arrived. I was nineteen, into my third year at The Cooper Union for the Advancement of Science and Art in New York City. The notice was from the United States Army, stating that I was being drafted—drafted into the army. Into World War II. It was early spring, 1943, and I had had a sense that my notice would be coming soon; many friends at Cooper Union had already been drafted, as had a number of fellows in my Bronx neighborhood. If you were over the age of eighteen in 1943, you expected a draft notice. When I went home and told my mother, she had an unexpected reaction. She said, "Son, what will you do when there's no icebox door for you to pull open every five minutes?"

April 23, 1944

When I left Cooper for the army Eva I had a fairly strong grasp of the basic war issues. I had worked on the school's war board as director and had come in contact with students from most of the main N.Y. colleges at meetings and discussion groups. The theme was always ~~how~~ what is the student doing to help win the war and how can he do more.

I can thank those meetings for a broad outlook which was easily able to overcome the ready cynicism of so many friends. I think that that was the reason why it was so easy for me to adapt my interests within the framework of army life.

↑ **April 23, 1944**
When I left Cooper for the army Eva I had a fairly strong grasp of the basic war issues. I had worked on the school's war board as director and had come in contact with students from most of the main N.Y. colleges at meetings and discussion groups. The theme was always what is the student doing to help win the war and how can he do more.

I can thank those meetings for a broad outlook which was easily able to overcome the ready cynicsism of so many friends. I think that that was the reason why it was so easy for me to adapt my interests within the framework of army life.

WHEN I LEFT Cooper Union for the army, I had a fairly strong grasp of the basic war issues. I had worked on the school's war board and had met with students from other New York colleges to discuss what more the students could do to help with the war effort. The war had begun four years earlier when Germany invaded Poland. Germany's ruler, Adolf Hitler, together with the Nazi Party, were determined to take control of all of Europe. Equally determined to stop them, the United Kingdom and France declared war on Germany. As more countries became involved and took sides, the world was split into two groups: the Allies and the Axis. The main Allied countries were the United Kingdom, France, the Soviet Union, China, and the United States. The main Axis countries were Germany, Italy, and Japan.

While Germany sought power over Europe, Hitler and the Nazis also aimed to create what they believed was a "master"

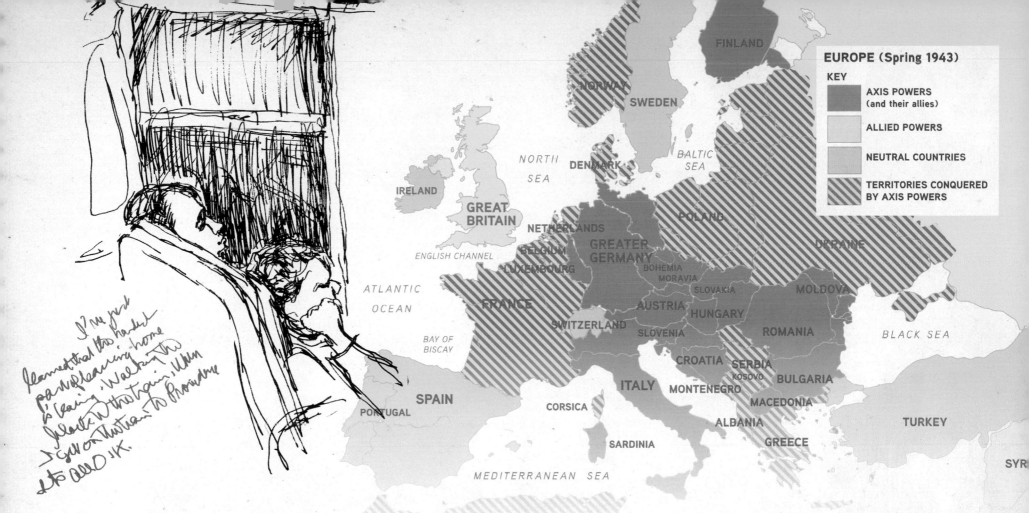

EUROPE (Spring 1943)
KEY

AXIS POWERS (and their allies)

ALLIED POWERS

NEUTRAL COUNTRIES

TERRITORIES CONQUERED BY AXIS POWERS

FINLAND
NORWAY
SWEDEN
NORTH SEA
BALTIC SEA
DENMARK
IRELAND
GREAT BRITAIN
ENGLISH CHANNEL
NETHERLANDS
BELGIUM
LUXEMBOURG
POLAND
GREATER GERMANY
UKRAINE
BOHEMIA MORAVIA
SLOVAKIA
MOLDOVA
FRANCE
AUSTRIA
HUNGARY
ATLANTIC OCEAN
SWITZERLAND
SLOVENIA
ROMANIA
BLACK SEA
BAY OF BISCAY
CROATIA
SERBIA
KOSOVO
BULGARIA
ITALY
MONTENEGRO
MACEDONIA
SPAIN
CORSICA
ALBANIA
GREECE
TURKEY
PORTUGAL
SARDINIA
SYR
MEDITERRANEAN SEA

racc—and many groups of people did not fit into the Nazis' ideal. People were targeted and often killed because of their ethnicity, religion, sexual orientation, and mental and physical disabilities. Jews were the most heavily targeted group, with nearly 6 million killed throughout the war, in one of history's darkest events: the Holocaust.

By the summer of 1941, Germany had invaded France, Norway, Belgium, the Netherlands, Luxembourg, Denmark, Greece, Yugoslavia, and the Soviet Union. The United States joined the war later that same year after Japan bombed Pearl Harbor on December 7, declaring war on Japan and the Axis powers the very next day. And just over a year later, I was to learn everything I did *not* know about war as I joined more than twelve million other American soldiers in what would be the largest war in world history.

↖ I've just learned that the hardest part of leaving home is leaving. Walking the block to the train. When I get on the train to Providence it's all O.K.

"Whites on one side, Blacks on the other."

JUST A FEW short weeks after that, I found myself in a railway station in New York City, at the military induction center. The recruits mingled. Suddenly a command came over the loudspeaker: "Whites on one side. Blacks on the other." I stood stock-still. A Black recruit nudged me. "C'mon, man," he said. "You Black, you know!"

The sky, the sunlight—they enclosed us all equally. But the United States's policy of segregation—dominant in the southern states, and now, I was to learn, in the US military—separated white people from Black people. While I had experienced prejudice in my lifetime growing up in the north, I had never experienced segregation before. And now, as a Black soldier, I found myself facing unequal treatment in a war that Blacks hoped would lead our nation closer to its professed goal of equal treatment for all.

As a child I was blithely unaware of any sort of segregation. My schools in the Bronx weren't segregated. Plus, I was too busy drawing, drawing, drawing. My parents had given me a little footlocker into which I would save my best work. My teachers encouraged my artwork, getting me every supply I could need. From elementary (PS 2), to Benjamin Franklin Junior High School, to Theodore Roosevelt High School, I was praised for my efforts. Though my teachers were all white, their focus was only on developing my art, drawing, painting, and block printing. At the end of high school, they encouraged me to continue my studies and helped me prepare a strong portfolio of my artwork. This inspired a dream: I hoped to win a scholarship to an art college. Without a scholarship, I could not go further.

CONFIDENT IN MY abilities, and in my portfolio, I applied to art colleges in New York. My dream, however, was quickly shattered. When my portfolio was reviewed at one school, I was told, "This is the best portfolio we have seen, but it would be a waste to give a scholarship to a colored person." The interviewer then described areas in the graphic arts field from which I was excluded.

My high school art teachers were as surprised as I was to hear this. So when I graduated in January of 1940, they said, "Ashley, come back and help us with the senior yearbook. In the summer, take the exam for The Cooper Union. They DO NOT SEE you there." I learned that what they meant was that Cooper Union administered its scholarships in a blind test: You put your work—sculpture (Plasticine clay), drawing, and architecture exercises—on a tray, and it alone was judged by the art professors. They never saw you. If you met the requirements, tuition was free.

"They do not see you there."

I was overjoyed when I learned that I passed the exams for entering Cooper Union. Free tuition! It was then that I decided to study art as my life's profession. I had no idea at that time that my life's profession would be what would help me survive the brutality of what was to come during World War II.

This certainly wasn't what I was thinking about once I got over my shock at having to go to the "Black" side of the railway station. I was prepared to create art, but I was not ready for the discrimination that I was about to face.

Ashley Bryan

1938

I was the first Black to be registered at St. John's Evangelical Lutheran Church.

ME WITH MY MA AND DAD
AND OLDER BROTHER SIDNEY

AS AN ADULT I found out that when I was a young child, I was the first Black to be registered at St. John's Evangelical Lutheran Church in the Bronx. Only recently I learned, from the son of the Sunday School superintendent, that his *father* had been the one to register me because the Sunday School registrar threatened to resign rather than admit a Black child. But as said, I was too busy drawing to notice any of this back then.

Even as a hopeful student, my college application experience had not prepared me for segregation, and the more active prejudice, that I was about to encounter in the army. Now I had to take a physical and psychological test to see if I was fit to serve. Many men hoped that they would fail these tests, for then they would not have to go to war. I passed!

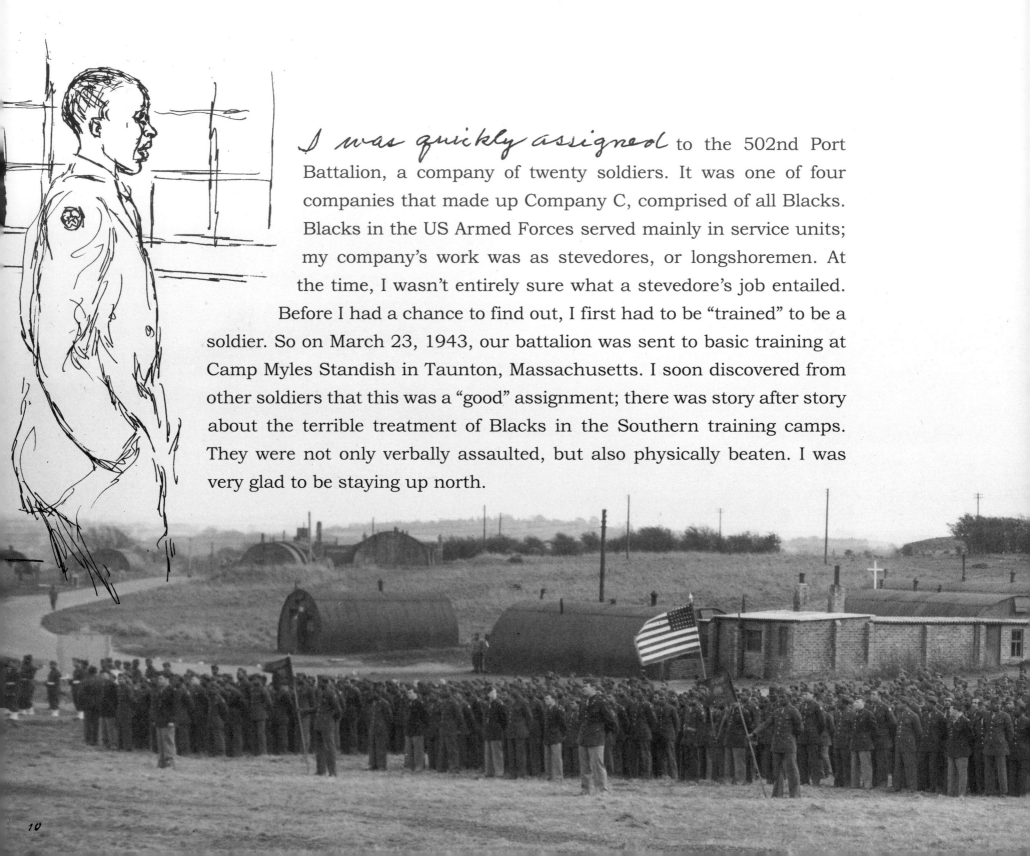

I was quickly assigned to the 502nd Port Battalion, a company of twenty soldiers. It was one of four companies that made up Company C, comprised of all Blacks. Blacks in the US Armed Forces served mainly in service units; my company's work was as stevedores, or longshoremen. At the time, I wasn't entirely sure what a stevedore's job entailed. Before I had a chance to find out, I first had to be "trained" to be a soldier. So on March 23, 1943, our battalion was sent to basic training at Camp Myles Standish in Taunton, Massachusetts. I soon discovered from other soldiers that this was a "good" assignment; there was story after story about the terrible treatment of Blacks in the Southern training camps. They were not only verbally assaulted, but also physically beaten. I was very glad to be staying up north.

AT CAMP MYLES STANDISH, we were housed in Quonset huts, rounded buildings so lightweight they could be lifted and moved with ease. My fellow recruits and I were regularly called out for calisthenics, marching drills, and hikes. Most of all, we were given training in automatically responding to orders and in acting as a group. To turn right, turn left, turn right again—it bored me terribly. To survive this boredom, I drew and drew whenever I could.

Three months later, basic training ended and the recruits were given ranks: private, corporal, technical sergeant, sergeant. Why I was rated tech sergeant (the highest rank a Black person could be assigned), 4th class, winch operator, I do not know. I didn't even know what a winch *was*. And I was terrible with machinery.

↖ Me seen through a magnifying mirror
May 20, 1943

← This is me, Ashley looking like somebody or something else. Hello everyone
Ashley

April 10 '43

The boys are singing in the
back of the barrack. Its Sat.
night and just a few of them
are here. They are singing Negro
Spirituals. Swell harmony. It
makes me feel so good @ hear them
sing these spirituals. When I hear
them sing some of the sad ones I
just shut my eyes and cry my
self.

← April 10 '43
The boys are singing in the back of the
barrack. Its Sat. night and just a few of
them are here. They are singing Negro
spirituals. Swell harmony. It makes me
feel so good to hear them sing these
Spirituals. When I hear them sing some
of the sad ones I just shut my eyes and
cry to my self.

Some of the men in my company had worked as longshoremen on docks unloading all the cargo from ships or freight cars. This, I found out, was very similar to a stevedore's work. They were familiar with all the gear of dock work and were used to operating the winches that lifted huge pallets of goods from ship to dock or dock to ship. I hoped they would show me the ropes. My colleagues started by explaining what a winch was—a mechanical device consisting of a hand crank and a spool, around which a metal cable or rope was coiled. The winch was used to pull in or let out tension of the rope or cable that secured the supplies being lifted when all was in place on the pallet.

Today I was 'baptized by fire'. War is Hell. And this was only a simulated affair. I had to crawl on my stomach a long distance with machine guns shooting over my head. And mines exploding on all side of me. I wasn't scared at first but after the mines and bullets started I was scared as hell. I thought I'd never reach the trenches. Some of the boys were so afraid that they just froze.

I eat more dirt and grass than I ever did. I didn't care. I breathed dirt. And those mines were so tightly strung with barbed wire that many of them was almost crawled into them. Once I was right next to one as it went off and the dirt covered me and pebbles pinged on my helmet and I swore bullets were hitting me. I crawled faster.

I was exhausted when I reached the first trench. My gas mask was loose and was pushing on everything. It held me back. I took it off and threw it in front of me and crawled after it. I finally reached the second and last trench and was covered with dirt and panting. I spat dirt. Dirt was on me and on me. I felt like crying when I thought of women of boys and girls and babies crawling crawling through the real thing.

War is Hell.

← June 26, 1943

Today I was 'baptized by fire' War is Hell.
And this was only a simulated affair. I had
to crawl on my stomach a long distance
with machine guns shooting over my
head. And mines exploding on all sides of
me. I wasn't scared at first but after the
mines and bullets started I was scared
as hell. I thought I'd never reach the
trenches. Some of the boys were so afraid
that they just froze.

I eat more dirt and grass than I ever
did. I didn't care. I breathed dirt. And
those mines were so tightly strung with
barbed wire that many of us almost
crawled into them. Once I was right next
to one as it went off and the dirt covered
me and pebbles pinged on my helmet and
I swore bullets were hitting me. I crawled
faster.

I was exhausted when I reached the
first trench. My gas mask was loose and
was hooking on everything. It held me
back. I took it off and threw it in

front of me and crawled after it. I finally
reached the second and last trench and
was covered with dirt and panting. I spat
dirt. Dirt was in me and on me. I felt like
crying when I thought of war and of boys
and girls and babies crawling crawling
through the real thing.

War is Hell.

↘ Under canvas they are sleeping.
Oh the cold
Oh the cold.

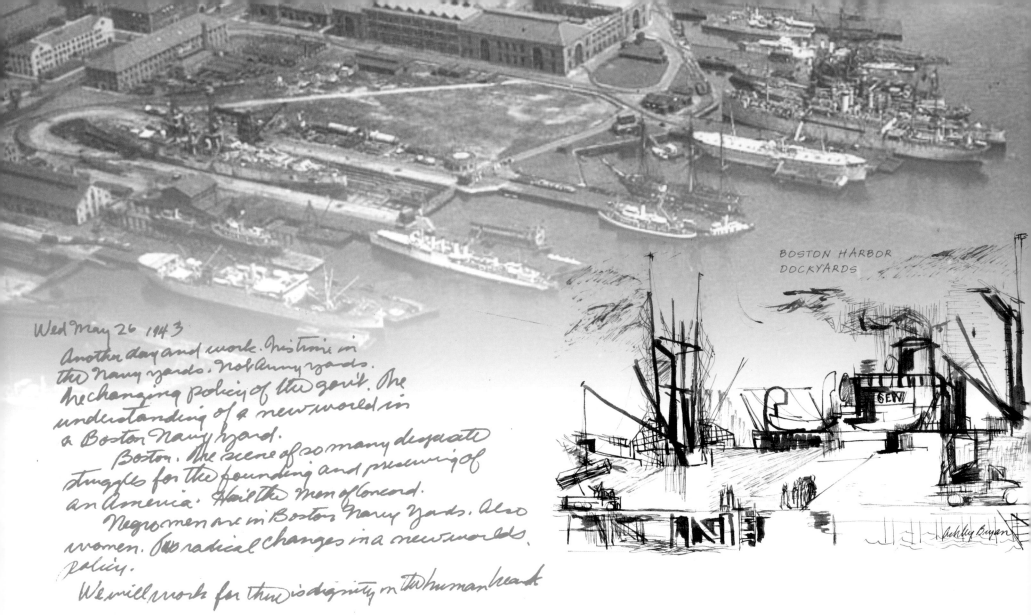

BOSTON HARBOR
DOCKYARDS

Wed May 26 1943
Another day and work. This time in
the Navy yards. Not Army yards. The
changing policy of the gov't. The
understanding of a new world in
a Boston Navy yard.
Boston. The scene of so many desperate
struggles for the founding and preserving of
an America. Hail the Men of Concord.
Negro men are in Boston Navy Yards. Also
women. Two radical changes in a new worlds.
policy.
We will work for there is dignity in the human heart

↑ Wed May 26 1943
Another day and work. This time in
the Navy yards. Not Army yards. The
changing policy of the government.
The understanding of a new world in
a Boston Navy yard.
   Boston. The scene of so many
desperate struggles for the founding
and preserving of an America. Hail
the Men of Concord.
   Negro men are in Boston Navy
Yards. Also women. Two radical
changes in a new worlds policy.
   We will work for there is dignity in
the human heart.

WITH BASIC TRAINING over, the 502nd Port Battalion was
stationed in Boston. We immediately began to work in the Boston
Harbor dockyards, handling all manner of army freight: huge
stackings on pallets of everything from guns and ammunition, to
food, to even jeeps and tanks. The winch operator—me!—was in
charge of raising and lowering the winch. I still couldn't imagine
why I was chosen for this job.

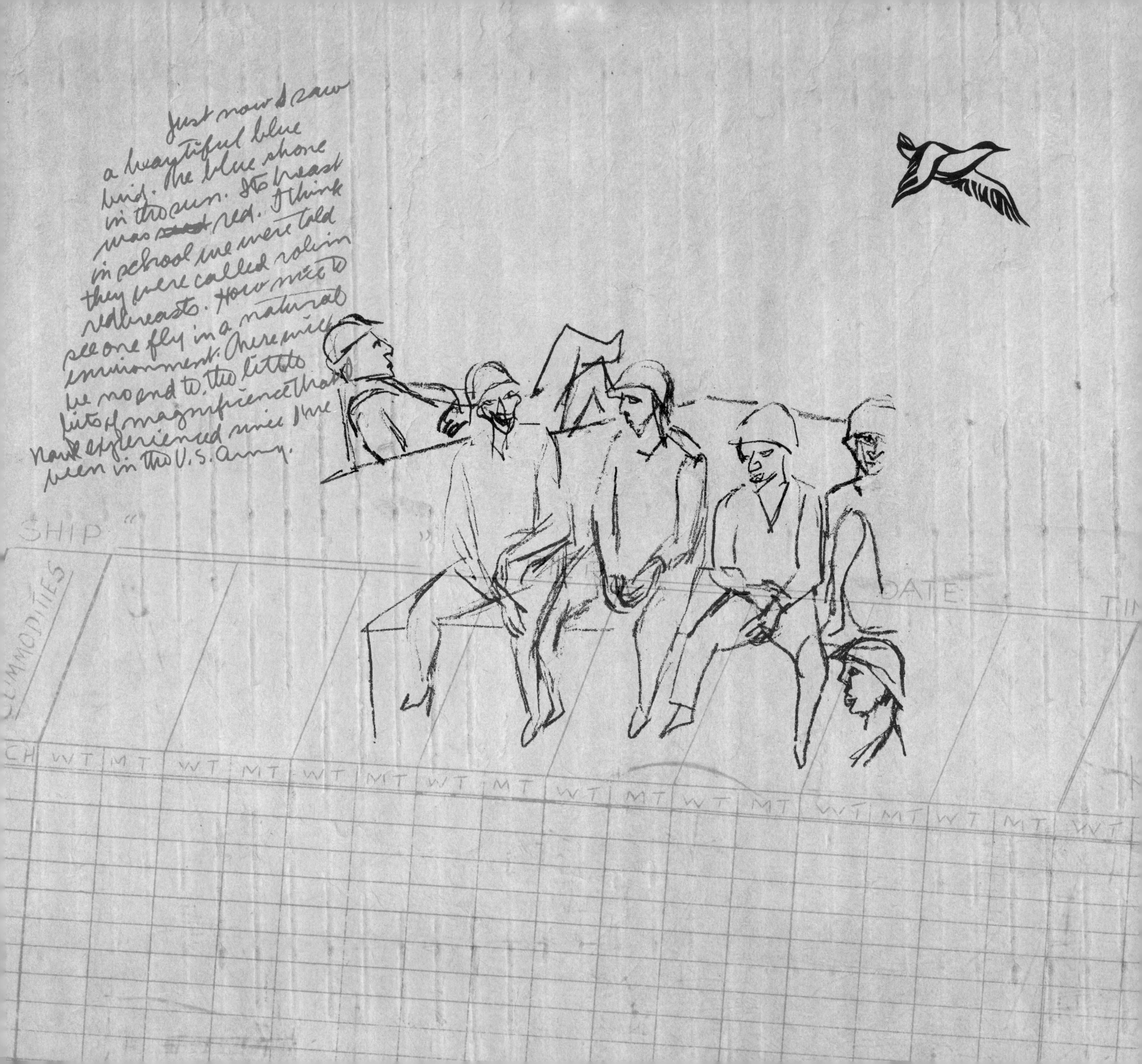

Just now I saw
a beautiful blue
bird. The blue shone
in the sun. Its breast
was red. I think
in school we were told
they were called robin
redbreasts. How nice to
see one fly in a natural
environment. There will
be no end to the little
bits of magnificence that I
have experienced since I've
been in the U.S. Army.
SHIP
COMMODITIES
DATE
WT MT WT MT WT MT WT MT WT MT WT MT WT MT WT MT WT

sunday may 23 1943
For twelve hours loading and unloading. Unloading freight cars on the dock and booms swinging and winches creaking. Night shift. Now I'm back. I went to sleep and I am so mad that I overslept. I couldn't help it I hardly have time to write a letter. I shall be more tried tomorrow and soon I shall just be able to work and sleep. Maybe a line to Ma now and then.

Its Sunday and I could only breath a prayer for strength to God. Thanks Lord for the past strength. For renewing me each day when I feel I can't go on.

GOD, make me brave for life

← Just now I saw a beautiful blue bird. The blue shone in the sun. Its breast was red. I think in school we were told they were called robin redbreasts. How nice to see one fly in a natural environment. There will be no end to the little bits of magnificence that I have experienced since I've been in the U.S. Army.

↗ Sunday May 23 1943
For twelve hours loading and unloading. Unloading freight cars on the dock and booms swinging and winches creaking. Night shift. Now I'm back. I went to sleep and I am so mad that I overslept. I couldn't help it I hardly have time to write a letter. I shall be more tired tomorrow and soon I shall just be able to work and sleep. Maybe a line to Ma now and then.

Its Sunday and I could only breath a prayer for strength to God. Thanks Lord for the past strength. For renewing me each day when I feel I can't go on.

GOD, make me brave for life

502 PORT BATTALION
Billeted in SOUTH BOSTON SCHOOLHOUSE   JUNE 1943

There are stars in all the windows and mothers are anxiously leaning on the window sills.
Sometimes I see a gold star.
And these stars are symbols of sons. And these homes with stars are American homes in July 1943.

WE WERE BILLETED in (put up in) an old schoolhouse in South Boston. I saw that some apartments nearby had stars in their windows. A blue star indicated that a family member was in the military. A gold star indicated a military death in the family. I wondered if they were doing the same thing in the Bronx. We took turns walking guard duty in front of the school. One morning it was my turn, and to my delight, the children who lived in the houses across from the school came over to investigate me. As I walked back and forth, back and forth, a carbine rifle on my shoulder, trying to keep a formal military posture, the children skipped around me, sang, asked me questions, imitated my pose. Aha! A survival tool! The children soon became my friends.

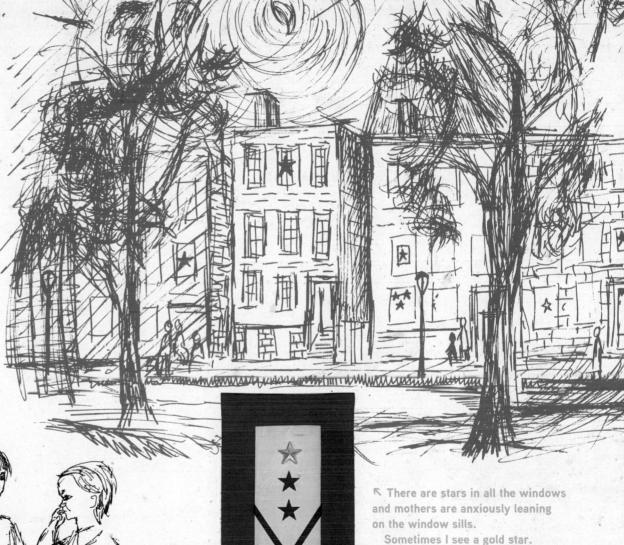

↖ There are stars in all the windows and mothers are anxiously leaning on the window sills.
Sometimes I see a gold star.
And these stars are symbols of sons. And these homes with stars are American homes in July 1943.

The little kids in these drawings live in the houses across from the schoolhouse where we stay. They are like all kids.

I'm going to work with them. I'll buy crayons and paint and paper and let them share my enthusiasm for work with ones hands.

Hobbies. Hobbies. Give them hobbies now. It will make strong cultural Americans of them.

I feel I have a big future in this neighborhood ahead of me. It will be fun.
God bless the little children.

ON MY DAYS off, I met with the children in the grassy vacant lot by the school. I brought crayons and paper with me, since many of the children had neither. As the children drew, I would in turn draw them and write their names on the drawings, or ask them to write their names. The children, as I do, loved to draw. I began to wonder if we could get permission to use a schoolroom for a summer workshop. Some of the children would walk the post with me, and the others would join in, trailing behind or swinging on my arms. One little boy wanted to go to college, he told me. He knows all about the war, things little children aren't expected to know. They would bring me fruit from their homes, and candy. When my daily duty was over, I bought them sodas. I know I violated every rule of the post. *Walk in a military manner, no meaningless chatter.* But they were my friends, and I was prepared for whatever the consequences. They made the guard-duty assignment a joy.

WED JULY 14, 1943
CHILDREN DRAWING
IN LOTS WITH ME

← Summer 1943
The little kids in these drawings
live in the houses across from the
schoolhouse where we stay. They
are like all kids.

  I'm going to work with them. I'll
buy crayons and paint and paper and
let them share my enthusiasm for
working with ones hands.

  Hobbies, Hobbies, Give them
hobbies now. It will make strong
cultured Americans of them.

  I feel I have a big future in this
neighborhood ahead of me. It will be
fun.

  God bless the little children.

DELORES

CATHY

JIMMY O'NEIL

JUNE 1943   REC HALL SCHOOLHOUSE. SOUTH BOSTON

23

Friday July 16 '43

I will write them. Robert (red) said if I were colored and big could I go with you. I smiled.

Why can't I get caloused to leaving my friends. I will have to do it again and again before this war is over,

↑ Friday July 16 '43
I will write them. Robert (red) said if I were colored and big could I go with you. I smiled.
    Why can't I get caloused to leaving my friends. I will have to do it again and again before this war is over.

79 W. Seventh St.
So. Boston, Mass.
August 3, 1943

Hello Ashley,
    This is Joe. I got your letter and was very happy to see it. I guess you have other friends down there. It is hot were to the beach ever day. I'm very glad you not far away. I wish you came back we had lots of fun with you. White soldiers have come over across where you were. But I like you better than every one of them. I hope I see you soon My far baby Francis is very fine. Write to me soon and don't this letter so long I love to read your letters.

Far too soon, eighteen weeks later, our battalion moved from the schoolhouse to a station closer to the harbor. I was sorry to leave my new friends—my time drawing with them was the best part of my week—but the children and I began to exchange letters. One of the boys, Joe, wrote, "I wish you came back. We had lots of fun with you. White soldiers have come over across where you were. But I like you better than every one of them."

¾ Sgt. JOE BEY

↓ June 14

Just finished painting Joe. I'll do some good things of him before this war is over. I could hardly control myself while I was painting him. I felt a mad sort of excitement and happiness. I rubbed the paint and used pencil and dug into the paint but nothing seemed to be enough.

I wanted to scream and toss my hands and bang my head. I wanted to tear up the paper and still have it. I couldn't. Too many soldiers around. I must control myself and my painting.

All the time a captain was watching me. I didn't know he was there. Didn't care. I noticed him when I finished. He asked to see something I did. Asked if I went to art school. Told him The Cooper Union, expecting it to fall on dull ears. He said Oh! The Cooper Union. New York.

He asked me to do a sketch of him. Pen and Ink. Any time he said. Just come in the dispensary. I will do it. I know I can.

June 14

Just finished painting Joe. I'll do some good things of him before this war is over. I could hardly control myself while I was painting him. I felt a mad sort of excitement and happiness, I rubbed the paint and used pencil and dug into the paint but nothing seemed to be enough.

I wanted to scream and toss my hands and bang my head. I wanted to tear up the paper and still have it. I couldn't. Too many soldiers around. I must control myself and my painting.

All the time a captain was watching me. I didn't know he was there. Didn't care. I noticed him when I finished. He asked to see something I did. Asked if I went to art school. Told him the Cooper Union expecting it to fall on dull ears. He said Oh! The Cooper Union. New York.

He asked me to do a sketch of him. Pen and Ink. Any time he said. Just come in the dispensary. I will do it. I know I can.

JENNY

JENNY

FREIGHT YARDS IN BOSTON

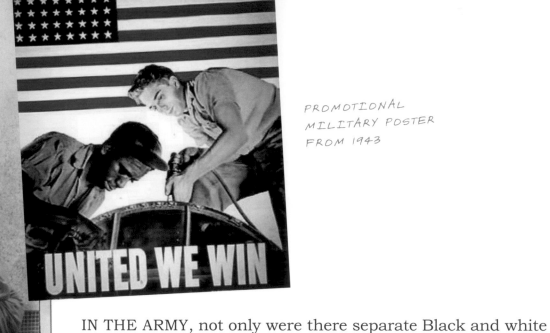

PROMOTIONAL
MILITARY POSTER
FROM 1943

UNITED WE WIN

IN THE ARMY, not only were there separate Black and white troops, but even when the troops did the exact same work, they were not permitted to do it together. Also, while Blacks were almost always restricted to service jobs—sweeping, cleaning, organizing—the white soldiers were given a much wider range of positions, as well as opportunities to advance. During basic training, all of the soldiers were given IQ tests. My score was such that I was offered a place in the Officer Candidate School, a rarity for Blacks. But I knew there was more to this than what was being said—I had already become good friends with my fellow battalion mates, and I sensed this was a ploy to break our comradeship up. The thinking was, by pulling one new man forward, the others would be resentful. But I'd never felt anything but deep respect for my fellow soldiers and for everything they were capable of that I was not. They had never resented or picked on me for my advanced schooling, in part because of my respect for them. I did not want to leave my comrades, men who accepted me. I declined the offer.

ME WITH A FRIEND

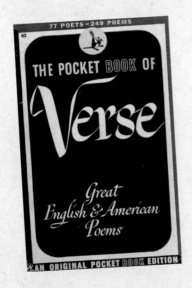

Additionally, I never thought about advancement in the military profession at that time, not at all. I just wanted to figure out how to operate a winch so as not to get in trouble. After months of working in the Boston dockyards, most of the 502nd had become a unit of experienced stevedores. All except me. I had no hand for working machines and found the loud rattling of the cables around the spool of the winch unsettling, for it was relentless; I felt I couldn't escape the noise.

I was initially one of two winch operators. We worked side by side, raising and lowering the cargo in or out of the belly of the ship that had docked in the harbor, all depending on whether the ship was bringing in supplies or being filled. A signalman would look into the hold where the supplies were, directing this operation.

Now, we were always to keep our eyes on the signalman, but I often had *my* eyes on a poem in a small paperback volume called a "pocket book" I held in my free hand. The signalman would holler and shake his hands frantically from above till he caught my attention and I could release the load from the top of the swaying boom to my partner's winch. That poor signalman would have become a nervous wreck if a fellow experienced winch operator

hadn't stepped in and taken over for me, saying, "Ashley, you go
and work down in the hold!"

In the hold of a ship being unloaded, there were cartons upon
cartons of ammunition, food, clothes, and medical supplies, all
waiting to be stacked onto wooden pallets and then hooked to the
cable that would raise the cargo from the floor of the ship onto the
dock. The men often worked in pairs,
chanting and swinging the cartons
into place. The steady rhythm of
singing and swinging helped us
save energy as we worked. I,
however, proved to be as
inept at keeping a working
rhythm as I was in running
the winch. It was a test in
concentration that I often
failed. I would sometimes miss
grasping the carton, causing
my partner to cry out, "Oh, my
back, my back! Aye, you go ahead
and draw!"

↖ Dear Eva,   August ? 1943
I found a swell library here in
camp. Thousands of books. All
the titles that I ever wanted to read.
I was so happy to find it. I dashed
to the art section and found many
many good books. Up to date books
and old established art books. I took
out a book of contemporary art first.

Well, I certainly welcomed this offer—I had already sketched many drawings of my fellow soldiers resting, because I chose to draw rather than rest. I could now add drawings of the men at work!

The officers, however, did not approve of my drawing, even in my free time. They wanted soldiers to look busy, even when there was no work to do. They said I "set a bad example. At least *look* busy, or we will put you in the guardhouse." But I couldn't stop.

I said, "Put me in the guardhouse now because I will never stop." There was no *law* against drawing, so the officers didn't know how to get around me.

→ So Eva, if ever you should bake make or find somewhere in your garden by accident or mistake some edible sweet of a more durable nature just remember your ole pal me (Ashley) who has shared with you the spiritual attainments in your kitchen or the nearest candy store and that a little physical reassurance goes a long way in making for a more two-sided enthusiasm. (hoo-ray for that!)

So long Eva. a few sympathetic tears for your marvelous dog and may you find happiness at last with a turtle.

So Eva, if ever you should bake make or find somewhere in your garden by accident or mistake some edible sweet of a more durable nature Just Remember your ole pal me (Ashley) who has shared with you the spiritual attainments in your kitchen or the nearest candy store and that a little physical reassurance goes a long way in making for a more two-sided enthusiasm. (hoo-ray for that!)

So long Eva. a few sympathetic tears for your marvellous dog and may you find happiness ~~with~~ at last with a turtle.

I had created a thick stack of drawings—over two hundred—when my battalion was ordered to pack up. We were departing Boston for an overseas assignment. Before we sailed, I mailed home the Boston battalion drawings and the ones of the Boston children. My parents saved them all in the small footlocker in my bedroom. Sadly, I lost contact with the children themselves for many, many years.

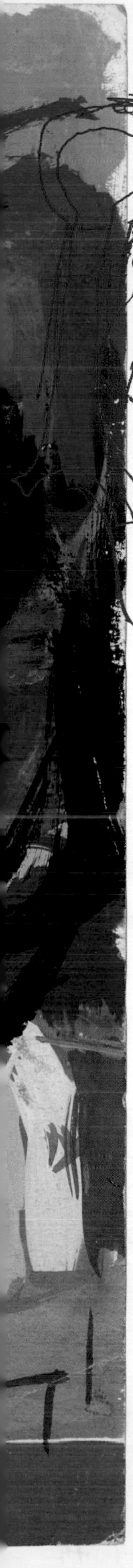

I would soon, however, have new subjects to sketch. Our destination turned out to be Glasgow, Scotland. We crossed the Atlantic by boat, arriving on October 19, 1943. Once settled in camp, we worked on the docks in the Glasgow port, doing the same type of manual labor as we had in the Boston dockyards. Though we were often tired at the end of the day's work, our energy would come surging back once we were off duty, because we looked forward to exploring the Scottish city and meeting the people. For most of us, this was our first time in a foreign country, so it was a great adventure. Yes, Scotland is an English-speaking country, but it would take time for us to become used to the Scottish lilt in the English language. I studied and loved the poetry of the Scottish poet Robert Burns. I memorized his poems that called for the Scottish dialect and shared them aloud, to the delight of my comrades. A favorite was "John Anderson my jo, John."

Camp - Scotland

THE SCOTTISH PEOPLE were warm and welcoming to all of us Black GIs. For some of the Southern men in our company, this was their very first experience of open, friendly encounters with white people. The Scots offered us an unquestioned acceptance as equals, a level of immediate friendship that we rarely received at home.

This did not please our white company officers, who were determined to enforce the US Army policy of segregation. Their general attitude that Blacks were beneath them—that "we do not treat them like that!"—prevailed. So they began to circulate terribly demeaning stories about Black people, saying that we would hurt them, that we had tails that would come out at night. Their goal was to make the Scottish people fearful so that they would avoid us.

To the officers' great annoyance, their efforts did not change the way the people of Glasgow viewed us. The Scots did not have the institution of racism—they weren't socialized against Blacks. Despite the officers' attempts to sway them, the Scots trusted our actions and friendliness rather than the officers' words.

We've got to have a chance. I look forward to that day when the lowest of the low and the highest of the high will have an equal chance.

So the officers took it a step further. We stevedores worked long hours loading and unloading cargo from ships, and now freight trains as well. Still, after work, we remained eager to meet with our new Scottish friends and do more exploring in the city. We'd clean up, and off we'd go. Then, one afternoon, we returned to camp only to learn that we were restricted and could not leave the premises. I soon discovered that the white soldiers did not have the same restriction placed on them! I found this terribly upsetting. Perhaps even *more* upsetting was realizing that my fellow soldiers weren't as upset as I was—the truth was that they expected to be treated poorly by the white officers, by whites, as that was what they had always experienced. For the rest of our time in Glasgow, we had to suffer the humiliation of asking for our freedom during the evenings, sometimes resulting in the restriction being lifted for a particular day, more often being told a flat no.

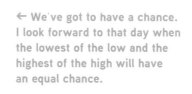

MOVIE POSTER FOR A
US ARMY PROPAGANDA FILM

← We've got to have a chance.
I look forward to that day when
the lowest of the low and the
highest of the high will have
an equal chance.

↑ Saturday May 22 1943
The seagul is a soul. It is my lonely
soul when I am down by the water
front. I can be a seagul down by
the water front. How much of man
is flapping for a moment and then
moving forward, motionless.

Scotland

GLASGOW SCHOOL OF ART

THE COMPANY OFFICERS may have restricted our socializing, but none of them were going to keep me from my aim to continue growing as an artist. Now, a new possibility opened up for me. I had already heard about the Glasgow School of Art, which lay in the center of the city. The building was internationally famous, designed by the architect Charles Rennie Mackintosh, an artist on par with Frank Lloyd Wright and whose work I admired. I decided to ask for permission to attend this art school. I'm not sure where I worked up such nerve!

I prepared a folder of my best drawings and presented it to my company officer, making my plea. My request was roundly denied as the officer shouted, "This is war! Get out! Get out!"

However, I had learned early on from my parents that if you are doing something creative and constructive, never let anything or anybody stop you. So I took my folder and met with the battalion commander, Colonel James Pierce. He looked through my drawings of the men handling cargo, of the men at rest, of the men at work, and was impressed. He gave me permission to attend the Glasgow School of Art. Colonel Pierce had an appreciation for the arts. He noted the men playing instruments and, realizing that he had gifted musicians among the stevedores, created the 502nd Port Battalion band. (This band later became the first band to ever perform from a foxhole—just after D-Day!)

The fellows in my company never held it against me that I was free to leave camp to go to the art school, even when they were restricted. I had always shared my artwork with them and had helped some of them write letters to loved ones at home, so they were glad for me, glad that I had a chance to get better at something I loved. For while they were playing cards or dice, I was drawing, drawing, drawing. They also took it as my way of going over the head of our company officer, and cheered me on.

↑ May 20 1943
This is one of the basic themes of the Human Comedy. The musical background to the picture was so unearthly beautiful and when I think about it and hear it to myself everything tightens up inside.

Dear Eva   December 25 1943

It's Christmas Morning. Christmas morning. The boys are all sitting near a stove at the gate waiting for the busses to come to take us to work.

They are saying Merry Xmas and are talking about what they were doing last year at this time. Some of them are just sitting with their heads in their hands. They are thinking Eva or dreaming and they are silent and are saying nothing.

The stars are still and will be still for a few more hours in this morning in Great Britain

December 25 1943

← Dear Eva

It's Christmas Morning. Christmas morning. The boys are all sitting near a stove at the gate waiting for the busses to come to take us to work.

They are saying Merry Xmas and are talking about what they were doing last year at this time. Some of them are just sitting with their heads in their hands. They are thinking Eva or dreaming and they are silent and are saying nothing.

The stars are still and will be still for a few more hours in this morning in Great Britain.

I had enrolled in a basic drawing class at the Glasgow School of Art. At Cooper Union, we drew from live models. Here, the classes used plaster copies of Greek and Roman antique statues as models, classical drawing in a formal, academic style. Though I was already using a more progressive style in my work, I did not feel constrained in the new classes. I practiced the assigned formal renderings, then I surprised my fellow students with the more free and open drawings I would do afterward. I became good friends with many of them, and they often invited me to join them on visits to art galleries and to cultural programs in the city. Remembering how

glad I was to receive fruit and candy from the children in South Boston, I in turn, on visits to my new friends' homes, would bring along goods such as canned fruits that I would buy at our PX (the "post exchange" that served as a store on our military base) that, because of war rationing, were unavailable to them.

↓ Dear Eva   April 23, 1944

At first I just drew Eva. I drew because it was so wonderful to be able to draw. and to have such a wealth of material. I didn't care what it was or where I was or on what I drew as long as I was able to take advantage of the new things that I was seeing.

I no longer draw anything but select what means the most to me and what best describes my relationship to it. This last change has come about within the last month and a half. After carefully studying the painting that I had done for the mess hall exhibition: It seems like such an obvious conclusion but it does not come about in the words and even now I have not fully realized it. Most important Eva there is direction in the work that I am now doing. More than ever I see the seeds of another work in the preceeding painting. This is good.

April 23, 1944

Dear Eva

At first I just drew Eva. I drew because it was so wonderful to be able to draw. and to have such a wealth of material. I didn't care what it was or where I was or on what I drew as long as I was able to take advantage of the new things that I was seeing.

I no longer draw anything but select what means the most to me and what best describes my relationship to it. This last change has come about within the last month and a half. After carefully studying the painting that I had done for the mess hall exhibition; It seems like such an obvious conclusion but it does not come about in the words and even now I have not fully realized it. Most important Eva there is direction in the work that I am now doing. More than ever I see the seeds of another work in the preceeding painting. This is good.

Alas, my studies and time with newfound friends came to too quick an end. There was a war on! Just a few months later, the command came to break camp and depart Scotland. I regretted leaving the art program and the friendship of the students. We had no idea of where exactly the coming assignment would be, just that we were heading for France. On June 2, 1944, we set sail to become part of the flotilla of thousands of ships headed for the coast of Normandy.

IT SEEMED THAT we had spent months and months preparing others for the war, but we were now going to be in the thick of it. We were about to join what was to become one of the most ambitious military operations the world had ever seen.

Nazi Germany, having already taken over Poland, Czechoslovakia, and other countries in Europe, was now on the verge of overtaking France. Paris was already occupied. They had only a few coastal cities left to invade, and then their next assault would likely be on Great Britain. The French Resistance was heroically trying to push them back. German officers, anticipating heated resistance at the coast, had heavily fortified the major French ports such as Le Havre and Marseille. They expected that the Allies would attempt to land at those ports to put up that anticipated resistance.

What they had *not* envisioned was the Allies landing all the gear needed to back up their invading army
on a *beach*,

so they did not suspect the massive operation the Allies were planning. They had *not* envisioned the invention of a navy-inspired vehicle called an "amphibious duck"—a vehicle that could operate as a truck on land and a boat on sea, which permitted the coast of Normandy to be chosen as a viable invasion spot.

AMPHIBIOUS DUCK

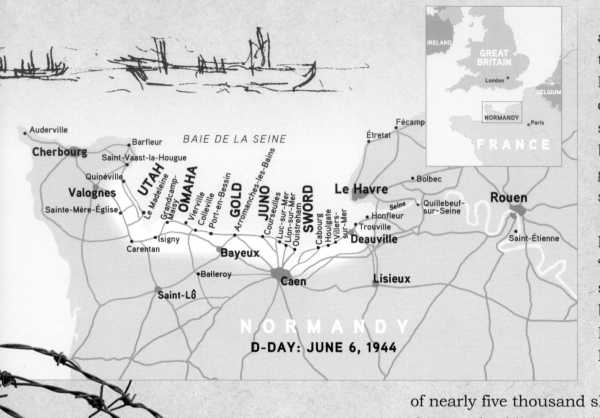

BAIE DE LA SEINE

Auderville
Cherbourg
Barfleur
Saint-Vaast-la-Hougue
Quinéville
Valognes
Sainte-Mère-Église
UTAH
Le Madeleine
Grandcamp-
Maisy
OMAHA
Vierville
Colleville
Port-en-Bessin
GOLD
Arromanches-les-Bains
JUNO
Courseulles
Luc-sur-Mer
Lion-sur-Mer
Ouistreham
SWORD
Cabourg
Houlgate
Villers-
sur-Mer
Le Havre
Étretat
Fécamp
Bolbec
Seine
Honfleur
Trouville
Deauville
Quillebeuf-
sur-Seine
Rouen
Saint-Étienne
Isigny
Carentan
Bayeux
Balleroy
Caen
Lisieux
Saint-Lô

NORMANDY
D-DAY: JUNE 6, 1944

IRELAND
GREAT
BRITAIN
London
BELGIUM
NORMANDY
Paris
FRANCE

Still, the Nazis were extremely thorough and took few chances. They buried thousands of land mines throughout the Normandy coast, making it exceedingly dangerous to land. They littered the shallows with barbed wire, and they also built pillboxes—small concrete dug-in guard posts—at intervals along the shore so that snipers could pick off infiltrators.

Yet it was imperative to get the hundreds of Allied cargo ships called "Liberty ships," packed with soldiers and supplies, onto the shore so they could begin making their way inland to help the French Resistance fight the Nazis and free Paris.

The plan was massive. A flotilla of nearly five thousand ships, filled with almost two hundred thousand soldiers, and hundreds more cargo ships carrying the enormous amount of supplies—from bullets to food to medical provisions—the army would need as backing for a successful campaign, sailed to several French beachheads. There they hovered off the French side of the English Channel. My cargo ship laid anchor off the Normandy beach we code-named Omaha.

At this point, we all knew we were planning an invasion, but we didn't know when it would actually happen. We were eager and anxious for the actual invasion to begin so we could unload all the cargo for the advancing Allies. A key part of the Allies' plan had to do with the weather. It was storming, with seas so heavy and winds so high that the Nazis never imagined that anyone would attempt to land in such conditions. That, combined with the belief that the beaches were impenetrable and thus impossible to breach, led their high commander, Field Marshal Erwin Rommel, to make a critical decision. He left France for Germany to visit his family for his wife's birthday and to meet with Adolf Hitler. Several other commanders took a break as well, leaving the beach unsupervised. Rommel hadn't expected a break in the weather. He hadn't expected the tenacity of the Allied forces.

But the Allies were keeping a keen eye on the weather. And sure enough, on the morning of June 6, 1944, the winds died down, the seas calmed, and a high tide and the command from General Dwight D. Eisenhower were what we needed to gain that most strategic of positions. Operation Overlord was to begin! We were soon just a few hundred yards from the beaches.

A ship Eva
the clean straight line of a bow. leaping
clear of the water
                 a ship
        to be loaded   Unloaded
for 1944. Today.   by us
The soldiers are working. Sweating
looking at the boxes they are unloading and stacking. labeled . . .
'From the United States of America. One
of the United Nations.' They are pray-
ing for Victory in 1944   Ashley

WAITING OFF THE BEACH

OMAHA BEACH, THE BEACH my battalion was to invade, was the most heavily defended of all the beaches. The very first thing that had to be done once we reached shore was to try to get the men safely across and to the mainland. This meant we had to clear the beach of the thousands of land mines lying in wait. This extremely dangerous task was left primarily to the Black quartermaster companies, and it had to be completed before the infantry could storm the beach. Black soldiers were ordered to use their mess forks to probe sand for anti-personnel bombs. Many Black lives were lost when mines exploded as they were being cleared, or when the mines were so well buried that they were accidentally stepped on and detonated.

The merchant supply ships waited offshore until it was safe enough to follow up with reinforcements. Even after the beaches were swept, nearly the entire first wave of soldiers storming off the ships was lost to drowning, mines that couldn't be detected, or to pillbox sniper fire.

It was when you saw bodies floating in the water that you truly *understood* what was happening. All told, more than 3,600 Allied soldiers, many of them Black, were lost on that first day on Omaha and Utah Beach. The fallen soldiers were buried in temporary mass graves, and it was again the Black quartermaster soldiers who were assigned this grim task. There was always a great hurry to clear the beaches so that the newly disembarking soldiers wouldn't have to see the devastation and lose heart. The fallen Black soldiers were often removed first; the news media there did not want to show Blacks in their newsreels.

More than 3,600 Allied Soldiers, many of them Black, were lost on that first day on Omaha and Utah Beach.

FEW PHOTOS OF BLACK SOLDIERS
CLEARING MINES EXIST, THIS
ONE WAS TAKEN IN ITALY.

STORMING THE BEACH ON D-DAY

I haven't been there for a long time but now I walk into the church. I walk far forward. remaining habit of confirmation days when we went to sit in the eyes of the pastor. Now I sit toward the middle, glance around. Smile in different directions. Then settle down to the duties of God.

I begin Dear Lord
the prayer I'd say to myself

Dear Lord.
That's all. breathe deeply. Think about the service. Then breathe deeply.
In the name of the father and of the son and of the holy ghost . . . 3 months now. here in this place. How do I feel. The months of foxholes and stress and the survival

Amen Amen Amen
Beloved is the Lord. Let us draw near
How close how close. near even now.

When there is no more than the morale binds[?], the prayers. The church.
Thank God I thank God for such a church for such teaching for the thoughts in recollection with a true heart

The urgency of it. The need of it
Xmas comes nearer. Began the thoughts of Christ
Christ. The Lord.
I must hold tight to a belief above the smallness of our [illegible] And be led by

the feeling of a strong internal power.
I write you now Pastor [illegible] because more than ever I call your name and need you now

↑ This is one helluva Dday+1. Its all so damn quiet. The ship is all rigged up. The first truck ready to come out and here its all so goddamned quiet off the french coast. The fellows are lying in the sun. Coney Island. P 38's pass and other allied planes come over this convoy in waves almost every minute. But no action. no nothing. Except that this morning one of the ships sunk and I cant explain how. It just blazed up. smoked. prow up and soon under.

We're about 2 miles out from the coast and the whole convoy is riding at anchorage. Destroyers weave in and out. Nothing else

. . . Don't know when we'll start to unload this ship. I'd feel allright if I were running that winch. I'm damn sick now of reading and lying in the sun and drawing— Let's get this the hell over with.
So this is France. This coast [illegible]

ON DAY THREE, however, we began madly unloading all the equipment from our Liberty ship into the amphibious duck. We then climbed down the ladder into the duck. Once it rolled onto shore, we scrambled off and took cover as it continued on to deliver supplies of food and ammunitions to the Allied troops advancing inland toward Paris. They had everything the soldiers would need for backup if they got a grip. This allowed those soldiers to be far more nimble, as they weren't encumbered by massive packs and conveyance vehicles—the ducks would catch up with them, let them get what they needed, dash back, refill, and start the process all over again.

My own company's first order of business onshore was to dig ourselves foxholes—a dugout six feet long, several feet wide, and a few feet deep—over which we were to erect a low tent. It was there that we would sleep and take cover from enemy fire. Digging these foxholes was treacherous in itself, as we were hoping all the while not to walk on or dig into missed active mines. Not everyone was lucky.

We used small collapsible shovels that were issued with our equipment. To me, the shovel was well named. Despite my efforts to keep it open, the shovel would collapse whenever I applied

any pressure on it! As soldiers in my company were soon
disappearing into the safety of their foxholes, I only managed to
scrape a few inches into the ground. That night, the Germans
began raining bombs down. This was terrifying. I flattened
out in my few inches as if I had room to spare. When
one of the fellows complained about living in a foxhole,
another soldier said "Listen, man, when you leave New
York, you're camping out!" Soon afterward, a friend,
David, made his foxhole twice as wide so I could
share it with him.

IN THE MEANTIME, everyone was frightened and concerned about what might happen because the German Luftwaffe (German Air Force) was constantly bombing the Normandy coast. So we sent dozens of barrage balloons into the air, floating them out over the sea and shore. These massive zeppelin-shaped floats acted as decoys to confuse the German pilots, affecting the accuracy of the Luftwaffe's night bombings of the Allies' installations on the Normandy beaches and our line of cargo-laden Liberty ships. The balloon cables were just as useful—they kept the Luftwaffe from flying too low, which also interfered with their accuracy, preventing the bombs from finding their targets. We prayed that this would continue to work and that we would be safe from the ongoing bombings. I drew those barrage balloons again and again, but only recently discovered that it had been a Black company that had set them up.

Our foxholes were our battalion's base on Omaha Beach. We stevedores went out to our ship each day to unload the cargo into the amphibious duck, keeping the supplies streaming toward the advancing Allied forces. The work was near nonstop; when one ship was emptied, another arrived to take its place.

OMAHA BEACH,
JUNE 1944

↑ K rations
3 meals for 5

For meals, we ate C-rations, of which there were only three variations: meat and potato hash, meat and vegetable stew, and meat and beans, all of which usually came with bread and a canned dessert. At night we slept to the searing buzz of the Luftwaffe as they flew overhead like mechanical locusts. We prayed they would not get past our barrage balloons.

This all sounds terrifying. And yet I gave up my fear of death, as did most soldiers. Everything—life and death—was so close. Either you walked on air or on the ground, but you decide. You came to the realization that you either lived or died, so you just walked. You could step right onto a land mine, or into the path of a bullet, or not, so you had to get on with it. Do your job. You couldn't continue living if you held on to such terrifying fear, if you feared your every move. So you think, *I live or I die.* And get on with it.

What gave me faith and direction was my art. In my knapsack, in my gas mask, I kept paper, pens, and pencils. I would draw whenever there was free time, intervals in work. I refused to sleep. I *had* to draw. It was the only way to keep my humanity. My sketches weren't only to record the day's happenings, but

"I live or I die". And get on with it,

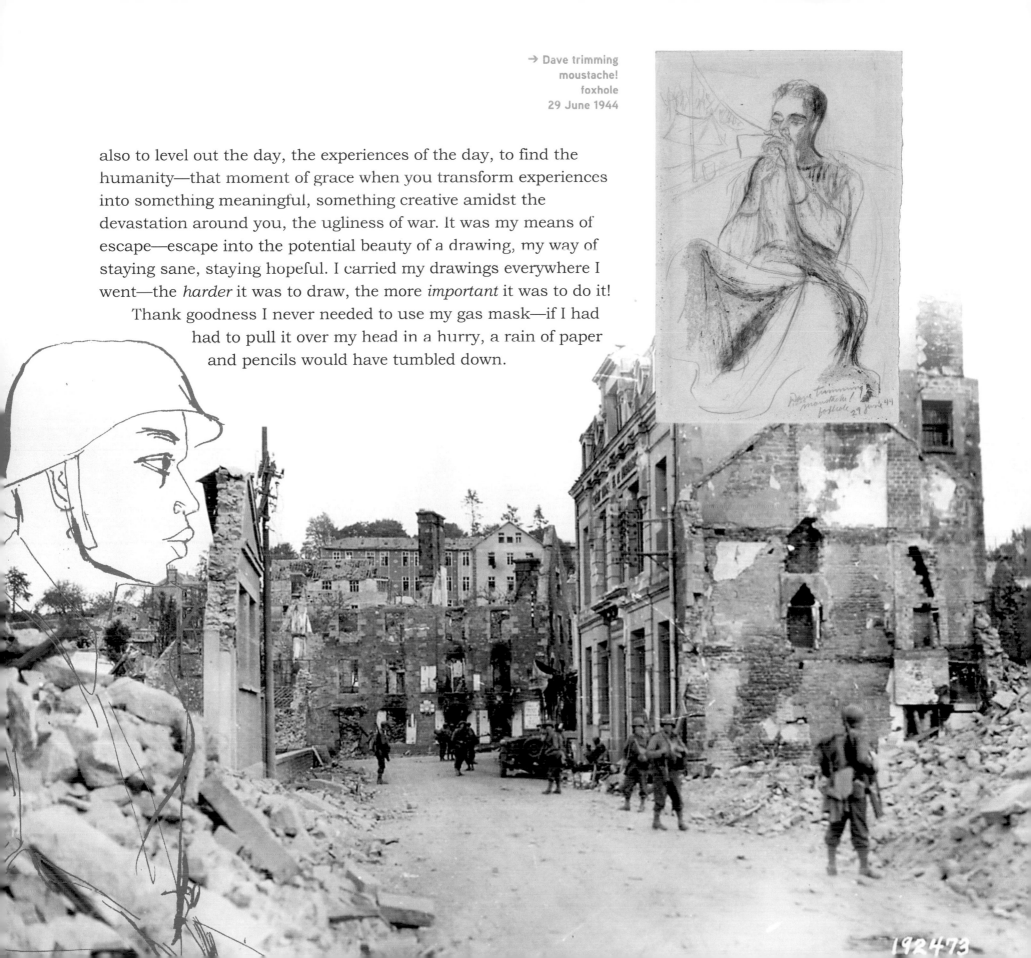

also to level out the day, the experiences of the day, to find the humanity—that moment of grace when you transform experiences into something meaningful, something creative amidst the devastation around you, the ugliness of war. It was my means of escape—escape into the potential beauty of a drawing, my way of staying sane, staying hopeful. I carried my drawings everywhere I went—the *harder* it was to draw, the more *important* it was to do it! Thank goodness I never needed to use my gas mask—if I had had to pull it over my head in a hurry, a rain of paper and pencils would have tumbled down.

192473

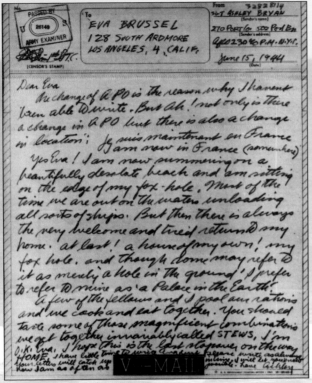

← Dear Eva,   June 15, 1944
The change of APO is the reason why
I haven't been able to write. But Ah!
not only is there a change in APO but
there is also a change in location;
  Je suis maintenant en France
  I am now in France (somewhere)
  Yes Eva! I am now summering on
a beautifully desolate beach and am
sitting on the edge of my fox-hole.
Most of the time we are out on the
waters unloading all sorts of ships.
But then there is always the very
welcome and tired return to my home.
at last! a house of my own! my fox
hole. and though some may refer to
it as merely 'a hole in the ground' I

prefer to refer to mine as 'a Palace in
the Earth'.
  A few of the fellows and I pool
our rations and we cook and eat
together. You should taste some of
those magnificent combinations we
get together invariably called STEWS.
I'm O.K. Eva, I hope this is the last
stopover on the way HOME. I have
little time to write Eva and please
write as always your letters will catch
up in time. I will let you know how I
am as often as possible.
  Love, Ashley

Whenever I could, I mailed a packet of drawings home to my parents, not because I feared something would happen to me, but because I feared something would happen to the drawings stored in my duffel bag.

As the Allies successfully pushed forward, driving the Germans back, our cargo ships emptied. In fall of 1944, the arrival of the rainy season turned the beaches to mud, and our unloading operations on the Normandy beaches ended.

↑ **Dear Cousin Eva   13 July 44**
There's a slight holdup in the work on this ship that we are unloading and I've taken the chance to leave the winch and fish out this V-mail from my gas mask. It's a beautiful afternoon because of the sun. Hot and friendly in spite of the underlying somberness of things.

I hollered across the hatch to the signalman for the date and he says 'the 13th'. 13th July. Its over a month now that we've been here Eva.

I've adjusted myself fairly happily to this fox-hole life . . . the sense of humor being able to lead the mind to the funny points in the gummiest of incidents. July 13—Come to think of it Eva I'm 21 today. My 21st birthday in France. When I was younger this was something I looked forward to. Now its here and I can't imagine what it was I expected of it. One thing—I can VOTE! . . .   Love Ashley

→ **Church at Colleville Sept 6 44**

14 November 44

→ **Dear Eva**　　　**13 Oct 44**
In a little while we'll be off to work.
It's raining and it's a long and
dangerous walk down steep hills
and un-mined fields to the part of
the beach where we are taken out
to the ships. Then the long dark
night, longer than ever, now that the
winter's long stretching darkness
has set in.

   I'm really writing you Eva now to
cheer me up. I've just eaten chow
and there's about an hour before we
leave. I feel low as hell and don't
want to think about it. If I lie back
and shut my eyes on my bed in our
little hut nothing but sad thoughts
play around. I'd better snap out of it.

13 Oct 44

Dear Eva
　　In a little while we'll be off to work. It's raining
and it's a long and dangerous walk down steep hills
and un-mined fields to the part of the beach where
we are taken out to the ships. Then the long dark
night. longer than ever. now that the winters
long stretching darkness has set in.
　　I'm really writing you Eva now to cheer
me up. I've just eaten chow and there's about
an hour before we leave. I feel low as hell
and don't want to think about it. If I lie back
and shut my eyes on my bed in our little hut nothing but sad thoughts play around. I'd better
snap out of it.

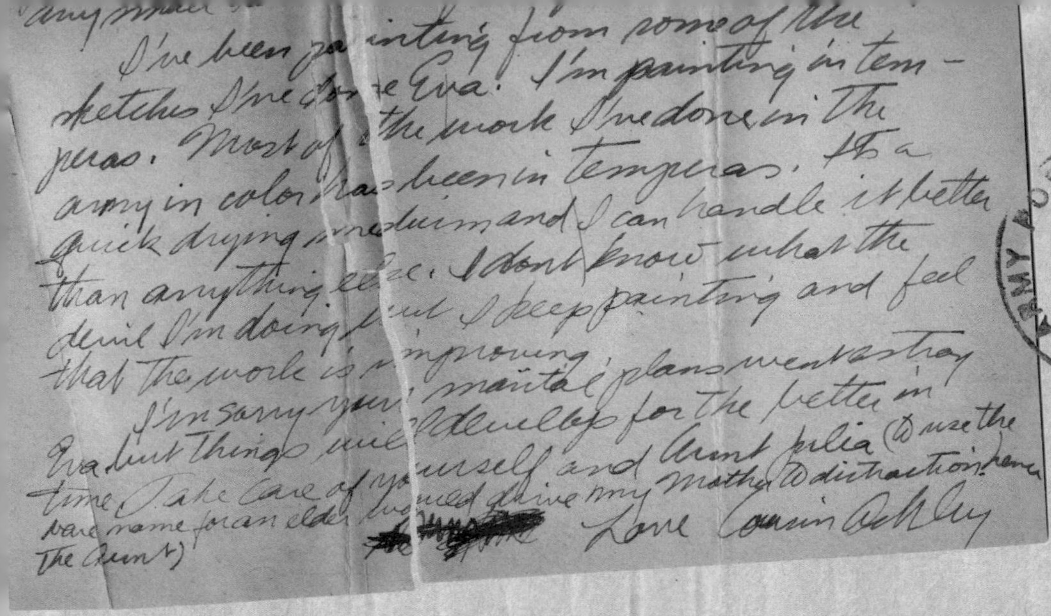

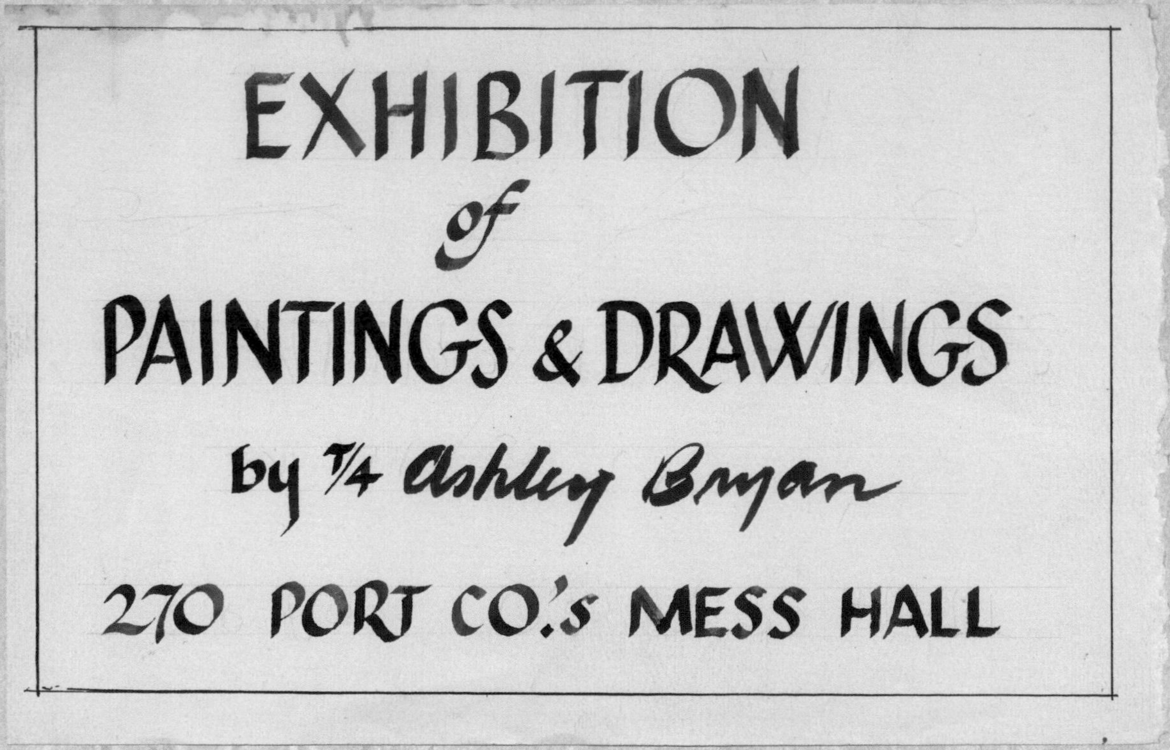

EXHIBITION
of
PAINTINGS & DRAWINGS
by T/4 Ashley Bryan
270 PORT CO.'s MESS HALL

← Nov. 1944 Le Havre
I've been painting from some of the sketches I've done Eva. I'm painting in temperas. Most of the work I've done in the army in color has been in temperas. Its a quick drying medium and I can handle it better than anything else. I dont know what the devil I'm doing but I keep painting and feel that the work is improving. [...]

→ 9 July 1945
He said he'd save it for always and when I became a famous painter he'd say 'Who Ashley? Oh yeah I know him. We were buddies in the old Deuce (as we call the 502). He painted this lighter for me'. Nates from Brooklyn. He's gone now. I hope he doesn't have to wait too long for transportation home. I gave him my address. Asked him to look up the folks. He says he's going to tell them how I ran the winch with one hand and read a book with the other and how I just painted through the invasion like it was art school, 'In a way of speaking' (Nate's favorite expression).

He said he'd save it for always and when I became a famous painter he'd say 'Who Ashley? Oh yeah I know him. We were buddies in the old Deuce (as we call the 502). He painted this lighter for me'. Nates from Brooklyn. He's gone now. I hope he doesn't have to wait too long for transportation home. I gave him my address. Asked him to look up the folks. He says his going to tell them how I ran the winch with one hand and read a book with the other and how I just painted through the invasion like it was art school, 'in a way of speaking' (Nates favorite expression)

67

By May 8, 1945, Germany officially surrendered and the war in Europe was indeed now over. But not, it seemed, for us. We had been sent to the debarkation port in Le Havre, east of the beaches. My company's focus shifted from emptying ships to guarding German prisoners of war. We were armed with carbine rifles, which we had been taught to use during basic training so many many months ago.

NORMANDY AMERICAN
CEMETERY AND MEMORIAL,
WHICH CONTAINS OVER 9,300
AMERICAN SOLDIERS

↓ Dear Eva   31 March 45

I came in tonight from the guarding of nazi prisoners of war feeling sick and tired and ready to sleep. On the way to my tent I was duly reprimanded by my section leader for my careless appearance on post, need of a shave. careless saluting. . . .

From a church friend's letter I read of the death of another member on one of our fighting fronts. For a long while the Church Bulletin listed no deaths, but the bulletins of the past months have listed one after the other of boys I was familiar with in church activities, whom I had been confirmed with, went to elementary school with, hiked with in the Palisades during the brief career of our boyscout unit.

This last person was well known to me. His family. A few days before I'd received a letter from his brother. Then there are the Cooperites. Architect named Rudy, good friend of mine. He was in France too a while. up front. He's in the States now, still living, getting better. And Henry in the Engineering dep't, still living. The Negro fellow. getting better. In Italy fragments tore into and through him from a German gun.

This is really slight Eva, nothing. But for me this is the toll. The hundreds of thousands. These are what make printers ink numbers real. This is the closeness. the heartsickness. The only real count.

This section leader says something was wrong with my cot during the day's inspection . . . the toll. The real count . . . books on your bed. mess gear wrongly displayed [...]

↙ Le Président Roosevelt est Morte.
The way it came to France, in the
French papers. The way I saw it
first. The dark lined border, familiar
now, this type in enclosures. The
dark lined borders. The terrible
mounting of pounding inside beating
and deafening the sound of the
words. but always the sight of them.
The feel of them. The insurmountable
truth of them. The [grief] searing
the hearts core. The uncontrolled
moaning recurring moan.

Below: Franklin D. Roosevelt on the
day before his death on April 12, 1945.

Background: Allied leaders
(l–r) Henri Giraud, Franklin D.
Roosevelt, Charles de Gaulle, and
Winston Churchill in Casablanca on
January 24, 1943.

30 april 45

There it is now Eva. The nations of
the world together. heads together.
Working out some means of keeping
a Peace in the world for the centuries
to come. This is good Eva. It is one of
the most necessary steps taken in the
interests of world survival.

Over here Eva everything is in
ruins. I know this city to be just
an example of hundreds of others
throughout the warscarred world.
With the ruins of the city goes the thousands of civilian lives. With the taking of the city goes the thousands of
soldier lives. ruined cities, ruined
lives, lost lives. Thats the cost
that you dont add. These figures have
a strange ~~xxxxxxxxx~~ power of
meaning more than an actual count.
Their effect is far greater than the numbers.
This is not mathematics.

The people of the world are paying
this price now Eva. They are paying
it with their eyes open. minds
open. in defiance to fascist developments that seek by force to claim
their basic rights and needs. Having
experienced the extent of wars destruction they are determined to pay the
full price now and forever.

← 30 April 45
There it is now Eva. The nations of
the world together. heads together.
Working out some means of keeping
a Peace in the world for the centuries
to come. This is good Eva. It is one
of the most necessary steps taken in
the interests of world survival.

Over here Eva everything is in
ruins. I know this city to be just
an example of hundreds of others
throughout the warscarred world.
With the ruins of the city goes the
thousands of civilian lives. With the
taking of the city goes the thousands
of soldier lives. ruined cities, ruined
lives, lost lives. Thats the cost that
you dont add. These figures have a
strange power of meaning more than
an actual count. Their effect is far
greater than the numbers. This is not
mathematics.

The people of the world are paying
this price now Eva. They are paying
it with their eyes open, minds open.
in defiance to fascist developments
that seek by force to claim their basic
rights and needs. Having experienced
the extent of wars destruction they
are determined to pay the full price
now and forever.

Dear Eva   22 May '45

Now that censorship is lifted I can write you what I
damn well please without the restraint induced by
the incriminating eyes of an officer. How well I remember the pointed coldness I was received with after
several untied outbursts that had nothing at all to do
with military information. All I did was give a
most objective and impartial account of something
that happened to me and the fellows at the merciless hands of our officers in charge. After those outbursts
I usually discovered that I was restricted to the
camp area because Lt. so and so had found kittens
in my galoshes during an inspection and that I
should know perfectly well that according to all of
the rules and regulations of war kittens in galoshes
are strictly forbidden!

THE BATTALION MASCOT!

↖ Dear Eva   22 May '45
Now that censorship is lifted I can
write you what I damn well please
without the restraint induced by the
incriminating eyes of an officer. How
well I remember the pointed coldness
I was received with after several
[illegible] outbursts that had nothing
at all to do with military information.
All I did was give a most objective and
impartial account of something that
happened to me and the fellows at
the merciless hands of our officers in
charge. After those outbursts I usually
discovered that I was restricted to the
camp area because Lt. so and so had
found kittens in my galoshes during
an inspection and that I should know
perfectly well that according to all of
the rules and regulations of war kittens
in galoshes are strictly forbidden!

Our company was soon relocated again near the devastated French city of Rouen. The glorious Rouen Cathedral and many of the city structures were in ruins from the German bombings. It was here that we heard the devastating news that Hiroshima and Nagasaki were hit with atomic bombs that had the potential to destroy the world. With this came the remarkable news that the end of World War II was near.

Would we at last be going home?

→ Dear Eva,   17 Aug 44
Thanks to the final Victory in the Pacific the great sounds of moaning and gnashing of teeth by my friends as a result of my late letter answering has been considerably subdued [. . .]

[. . .] The final end of the war cuts off our prospects of the Pacific, Eva, and I can assure you that there are no tears being shed over that loss. The news of the final surrender came limpingly through and the hills of France is not the most ideally situated place for receiving news rapidly I am afraid. So although we were a little slow in catching on to just what had happened the news finally found its way up the steep hill to us. It is only a few days since that announcement Eva and although there was no wild shouting or even a mild shout for that matter there was a great sense of releif and quiet happiness here.

Now it seems only to be a matter of time and transportation before we will be home again. This time for good. There is the great fight for a lasting and workable Peace ahead. Since Peace is the only recourse remaining for a civilization that is at last far too developed in the means of extinction for its own good it seems that we will resort to it and make it work this time and for ever.

I dont know when I'll get home Eva but when I do I shall be two months roaming before putting my shoulder to the wheel and I shall roam to California just to make sure that you are real.
Love Ashley

The mushroom cloud from the atomic
bomb dropped on Nagasaki.

While, alas, I was not given a one-way ticket home at that point, I *was* given a pass to go on leave for a few days after so many months of nonstop work. I went to Belgium, which was a welcome break. The Belgians accepted us Black soldiers as human beings and befriended us openly, just as the people of Scotland had. Again, this was a huge contrast to the way we were treated by Americans, our own countrymen. The trip to Belgium was also an opportunity to buy art supplies, especially paper. I'd grown so desperate for materials to draw on that I'd resorted to using the flat squares of brown toilet paper we'd been supplied with.

Once back on guard duty in France, however, many thoughts came to me. During my travels from Omaha Beach through France and into Belgium, all I saw was destruction. Houses were destroyed.

↗ French sifting for coal
28 Nov 94 Le Havre

← Red felt turban
French forces
Negro

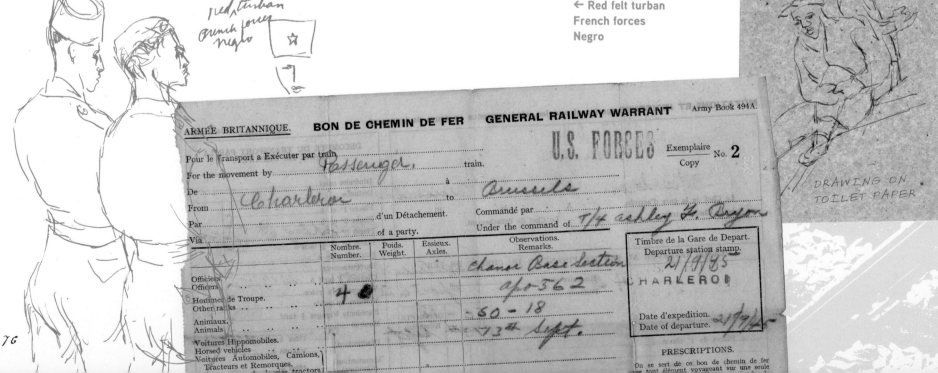

DRAWING ON TOILET PAPER

There's not too much difference between Rouen and Le Havre. That is Eva they're both ruins. The other day I was walking back to camp with a friend and I of a sudden looked at him ahead of me and said 'How casually we walk through all these ruins.' After I said it I was surprised it occurred to me and I felt a little foolish about having said it for as my friend said 'How the hell else can you walk through ruins after a year and a half of it.'

26 Oct 45

There's not too much difference between Rouen and Le Havre. That is Eva they're both ruins. The other day I was walking back to camp with a friend and I of a sudden looked at him ahead of me and said 'How casually we walk through all these ruins.' After I said it I was surprised it occurred to me and I felt a little foolish about having said it for as my friend said 'How the hell else can you walk through ruins after a year and a half of it.'

DESTRUCTION IN NEARBY CAEN. NORMANDY

The Rouen Cathedral was in ruins. Rubble was everywhere. People made shelters out of everything they could find. They were starving, and going through garbage in search of food. Now, back at the base, they would even jump on the trucks that carried the base's garbage that was on the way to be dumped. Our officers issued the command to shoot anyone who did this. Of course we did not obey; we attempted to help them in any way we could.

Still, there was a complete sense of desperation and despair. I came to the realization that, for the most part, the German POWs we were guarding were ordinary men, just wanting to go back to their homes, their families, their jobs. Then came another, more disturbing realization: The German POWs were being given more respect than the Black soldiers who had just fought for Europe's freedom. On bus rides to the PX in Le Havre, the German prisoners were permitted to sit up front with the white soldiers and officers, while we Blacks were segregated to the back, just like back home. And once at the PX, we were not even allowed inside.

↑ Side entrance
Cathedral Notre Dame de Rouen

SERVICE CLUB ★ UNITED STATES ARMY ★

80

THE 6888TH CENTRAL POSTAL DIRECTORY BATTALION
The only African American Women's Army Corps unit sent to Europe

The few Black soldiers who had been promoted to lieutenants out of necessity during the war were not allowed in the officers' facilities or clubs, despite having the same responsibilities as the white officers. We Blacks had risked our lives—thousands had *lost* their lives—to stop Nazism from spreading, to stop the Nazis' hatred and agenda of eliminating those people *they* had segregated out, deemed as lesser, as unworthy. And yet in many respects we were being treated in the same way. I knew that Black women in the war, working as Women Airforce Service Pilots (WASPs) and Women Accepted for Volunteer Emergency Services (WAVES), faced the same prejudices as we men did and perhaps worse. Where was *our* freedom? *Our* equality?

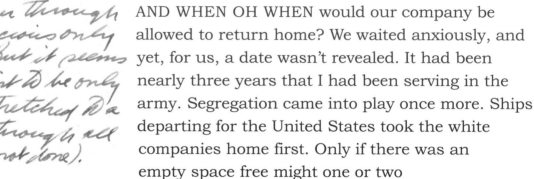

10 Sept 45

Dear Eva

I cannot remember when I last wrote you. Today is Sunday. a free day. I got up late and after much concern over the darkness of things I realized that I had not opened my eyes. That they were sealed by the cold in them. I rubbed them lightly for awhile and as if my eyelashes were tearing apart they opened weakly upon the bleak tent scene. whereupon I wished that I could sleep forever. forever through this dulling phase to become concious only again on the ships going home. But it seems now that what appeared at first to be only a matter of a few weeks has stretched to a matter of months and to sleep through all this time is impossible (or just not done).

AND WHEN OH WHEN would our company be allowed to return home? We waited anxiously, and yet, for us, a date wasn't revealed. It had been nearly three years that I had been serving in the army. Segregation came into play once more. Ships departing for the United States took the white companies home first. Only if there was an empty space free might one or two Black soldiers be allowed on those first departing boats, and _only_ if those ships had a segregated section for the Blacks to quarter in.

I had been put in charge of getting my detail back to the United States. So I traveled from port to port, trying to get my men a berth on a westward-bound ship, trying to get them home. And so it went, week by week, month by month, small groups of one or two or perhaps three made their way home—not to a reception as a unit, but in staggered, small groups without any fanfare, without recognition.

↑ Dear Eva   10 Sept 45
I cannot remember when I last wrote you. Today is Sunday, a free day. I got up late and after much concern over the darkness of things I realized that I had not opened my eyes. That they were sealed by the cold in them. I rubbed them lightly for awhile and as if my eyelashes were tearing apart they opened weakly upon the bleak tent scene. Whereupon I wished that I could sleep forever. forever through this dulling phase to become concious only again on the ship going home. But it seems now that what appeared at first to be only a matter of a few weeks has stretched to a matter of months and to sleep through all this time is impossible (or just not done).

→ 28 Sept 45

The next day news came that the battalion was being broken up. And then It came down as an official order. I was called in to help with the transferal of records.

That is now Eva.

The company is divided up.

After the years together. The close friendships. We wont go home. together.

Best friends are separated. on paper.

They started leaving.
We watched them leave
  watched them go
    gone.

Now there is a small part of us still left, and I am left until all the records are finished even though my group has gone.

George will probably leave tomorrow. Perhaps of all I will miss him the most.

There are just 800 soldiers (eight hundred). Once together in a unit. Now adrift. for better— for worse.

28 Sept 45

The next day news came that the battalion was being broken up. And then it came down as an official order. I was called in to help with the transferal of records.

That is now Eva.

The company is divided up.

After the years together. the close friendships. We wont go home. together

Best friends are separated. on paper

They started leaving.

We watched them leave
  watched them go
    gone.

Now there is a small part of us still left. and I am left until all the records are finished even though my group has gone.

George will probably leave to-morrow. Perhaps of all I will miss him most.

There are just 800 soldiers (eight hundred). Once together in a unit. Now adrift. for better— for worse.

IT WASN'T UNTIL January of 1946, when
my men were all safely sent home, that
I at last found a berth home for myself. I
arrived in Boston with the hundreds more
drawings I'd created during the war that I'd
still been carrying with me—the drawings
that gave me faith and direction during my
service. I took a train from Boston to New York,
New York to the Bronx. Once home, I knew only that
I wanted to complete my college studies in art at Cooper Union.
But I remained so haunted and devastated by recurring images
of the tragedies of war that I enrolled instead as a philosophy
major at Columbia University. I was hoping, in my naive way,
for answers to my now ever-present question, "Why does man
choose war?" Curiously, my diploma from Columbia was signed
by Dwight D. Eisenhower, then president of Columbia and later
president of the United States, and who had been the supreme
Allied commander of Operation Overlord.

"Why does man choose war?"

Before the war, whenever I'd sketch something, I'd use that sketch to paint from. But other than a few small temperas I'd painted in France, I closed my World War II drawings away, taking them out of the footlocker and putting them into one of my map-case drawers. This tall bureau of wide drawers was a safer way of sorting and saving this art. Only my family and close friends even knew that I had served in World War II.

THE LACE MAKERS
OF ROUEN

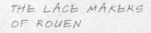

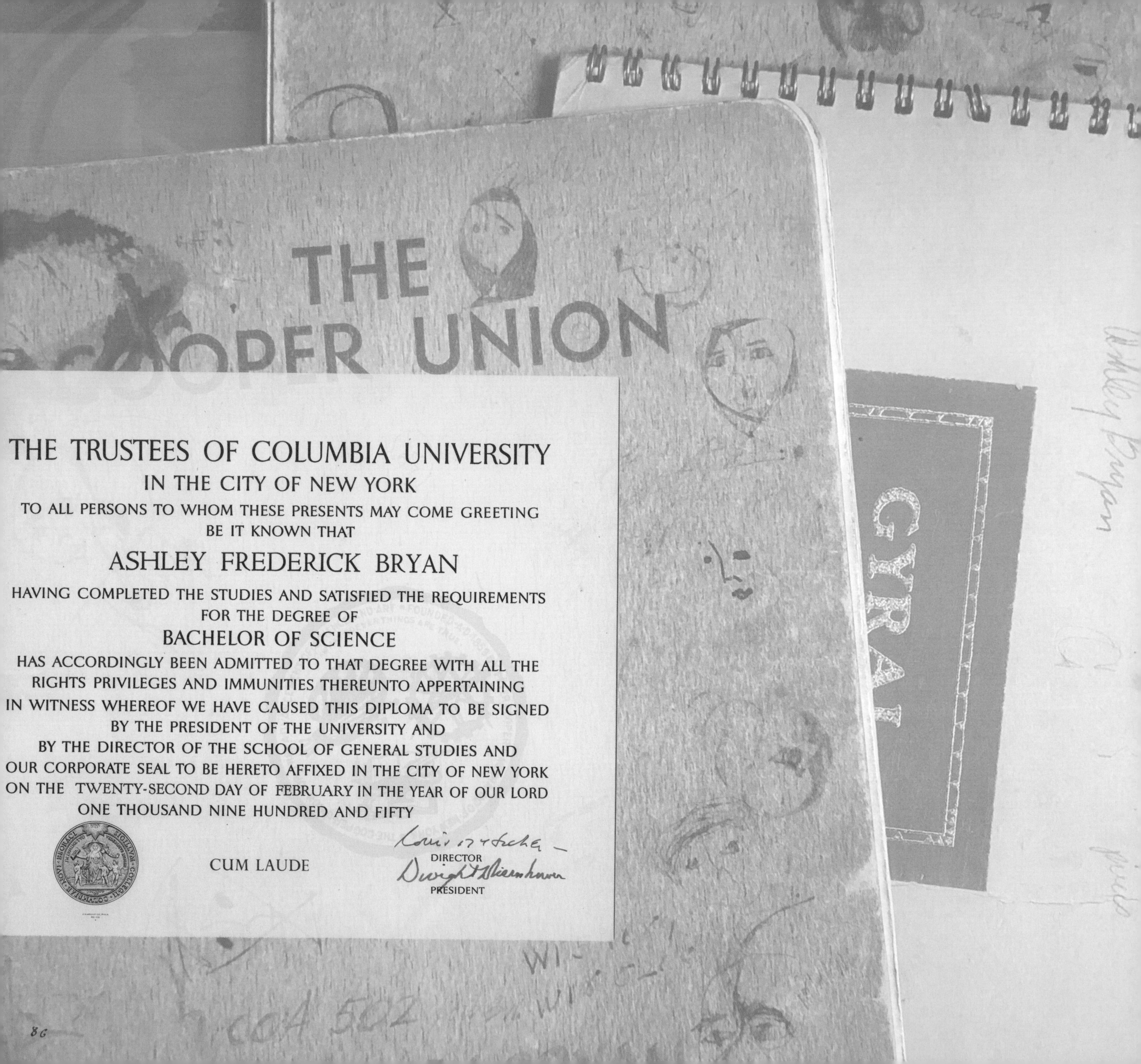

THE

COOPER UNION

THE TRUSTEES OF COLUMBIA UNIVERSITY
IN THE CITY OF NEW YORK

TO ALL PERSONS TO WHOM THESE PRESENTS MAY COME GREETING
BE IT KNOWN THAT

ASHLEY FREDERICK BRYAN

HAVING COMPLETED THE STUDIES AND SATISFIED THE REQUIREMENTS
FOR THE DEGREE OF

BACHELOR OF SCIENCE

HAS ACCORDINGLY BEEN ADMITTED TO THAT DEGREE WITH ALL THE
RIGHTS PRIVILEGES AND IMMUNITIES THEREUNTO APPERTAINING
IN WITNESS WHEREOF WE HAVE CAUSED THIS DIPLOMA TO BE SIGNED
BY THE PRESIDENT OF THE UNIVERSITY AND
BY THE DIRECTOR OF THE SCHOOL OF GENERAL STUDIES AND
OUR CORPORATE SEAL TO BE HERETO AFFIXED IN THE CITY OF NEW YORK
ON THE TWENTY-SECOND DAY OF FEBRUARY IN THE YEAR OF OUR LORD
ONE THOUSAND NINE HUNDRED AND FIFTY

CUM LAUDE

Louis Hacker
DIRECTOR

Dwight Eisenhower
PRESIDENT

GYRA

In a sense, I hid those drawings away just as I hid my experiences from those three years.

Most veterans don't talk. They want to live *past* the devastation and tragedies of their war experiences. It's so hurtful to put yourself back in those places. And yet they stay with you. Many veterans do not get the follow-up services they need. And despite the GI Bill that the government introduced to help soldiers get back on their feet after the war, there were many opportunities not open to Blacks. Whites received better loan rates for housing. They received money for education, for colleges that most Blacks weren't even allowed to attend. So it is therefore understandable that one-third of our veterans ended up on the streets.

Further, many of the Black vets from the war brought back the memories of how differently they had been treated by the Europeans. They came back home not wanting to reimmerse themselves into a world of prejudice, now knowing that that way of living did not have to be so. Part of the impetus and inspiration for the civil rights movement came from these soldiers, who began to stand up and inspire others to join them in their fight against unjust treatment.

↑ To Eva of George Carey
from Ashley
L'arc de Triomphe du
Carrousel
   June 1945
   Paris, France

I LEFT MY drawings in the map-case bureau for forty years. Yet I found ways to continue to study, to continue to grow as an artist. I returned to France, to Cezanne country—Aix-en-Provence—where I *could* study on the GI Bill. I was able to travel to Prades, a French town across the border from Barcelona, to hear the great Catalan cellist Pablo Casals perform again for the first time since the start of the war, when he had silenced his bow in protest of the Axis powers aiding Francisco Franco in overthrowing the people's revolution during the Spanish Civil War. He played in honor of the 200th anniversary of Johan Sebastian Bach's death. I drew Casals sitting by a pillar, conducting in the ruined Cloister where the musicians rehearsed. Unlike the war drawings, I had no difficulty using these drawings as a source for painting. I found I had

to draw swiftly to capture the musicians' movements as they rehearsed. This experience of swift, rhythmic sketching taught me that I need never be caught up wondering about style or concerned about influences. The intensity of this type of drawing gave me a sense of the rhythm of the hand in responding to the work that is the spring from which my art grows. If I tap into that, then ALL—whatever I create in whatever form—is related. Whether I create a drawing, a painting, a puppet, or a sea-glass panel, all comes from the same inspired source: the rhythm of the hand. Revealing aspects of the mystery of being human is life's inexhaustible research. Through the adventures of art, we find the meaning of our lives.

502nd Port Bn. site
Le Havre

"When I served in World War II..."

BY THE LATE 1980s, I was a published writer and illustrator of books for young people, living in Little Cranberry Island (Islesford) Maine. For over fifteen years, I was active in the children's literature annual seminar, Children's Literature New England (CLNE). One year CLNE chose War and Peace as the theme of their next symposium. I happened to mention, "When I served in World War II, I kept a sketch pad in my gas mask and drew on every possible occasion." A cry went up. "You! You were in the army?!" I gave the group a selection of my World War II drawings. Slides were made. At the following year's seminar, slides of my World War II drawings were projected on the screen. I spoke to an audience in tears. Now word was out to the book world that I am a veteran of World War II.

I then put those drawings away again.

← 502nd Port Bn. site
Le Havre

91

What I painted most steadily for the next several decades were the flowers that brightened the gardens on Little Cranberry Island, my home. There was beauty to be joyfully captured. Beauty to sustain me. Dahlias sturdy under ocean breezes. Irises straight and tall, reaching for the sun. Paintings of children and animals for the picture books. And after nearly fifty years of capturing beauty, I grew ready to open the map-case bureau to those war drawings again. For good, as an ongoing painting source.

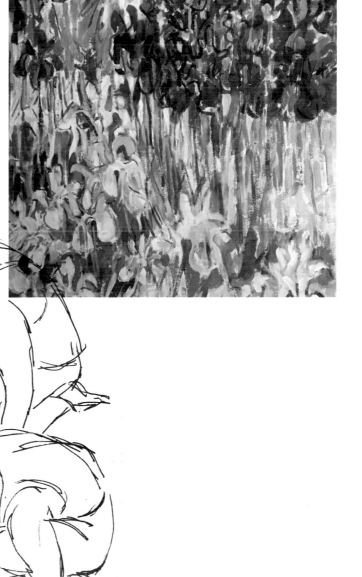

Recently, a committee of dear relatives and friends formed the nonprofit The Ashley Bryan Center. A museum exhibit of my life in art was planned. I was asked to do paintings based on the World War II drawings. I chose a few sketches to paint from as a start.

Fifty years ago, those paintings would have been dark—grays and blacks. But in really looking at those sketches now, I saw a beauty there—the beauty of the shared human experience. And I was able to face these sketches, face these memories and emotions, and turn *them* into the special world created by the men. I think of the men who were in the unit with me—I had such respect for what they could do, things I was so inept at. I remember their generosity toward me. I can never give them more than they gave me, so I would paint them in full color, filled with the vibrancy and life I had put into my garden paintings. I was ready.

I chose to paint from sketches of the soldiers playing cards or dice. This was a world they created, sheltered from the segregation and racism they endured. Sheltered from all sorts of war. I look now at the color, open form, and rhythm of those paintings. To me, they seem to have come out of my Islesford garden paintings rather than the drab colors of Omaha Beach! They have that surprise of discovery and invention that comes from seeing a well-known theme anew. They open the door to many other unexpected possibilities—because what is life, if not a voyage of endless discovery.

LAhCÈNE   AMED
10 yrs old   10 yrs old

Over sixty years after the war, I was scheduled to give a talk in Boston, at the Cambridge Public Library. I was reviewing my World War II drawings to send to a friend who wished to include some of them in her book about the overlooked contribution of Black soldiers in World War II. I asked my secretary to mail the drawings to the writer. On her own, my secretary studied my drawings of the Boston children. She located two of the children, now adults, and arranged for them to attend my lecture. Imagine my surprise when, after my talk, they introduced themselves! We are now good friends and I have lunch with them in South Boston whenever I am in town!

EXPRESSING GRATITUDE

It took an army to create this book, and my gratitude is enormous. Most notably, I wish to thank: Irene Metaxatos for her inspired design—a massive task handled with precision, grace, and beauty. Sonia Chaghatzbanian, who oversaw it all. Alex Borbolla for her unflagging diligence in too many ways to count. H. Nichols B. Clark, who—because of his brilliant gathering, sorting, and archiving of all my World War II art, journals, and letters—was always at the ready to provide documentation needed to create this book. Daniel Minter, who, with Henry and Donna Isaacs, coaxed forth stories I'd tucked away, and provided the impetus for the design. Jeannie Ng, who takes such great care of my every word. Elizabeth Blake-Linn, who ensures all of my books are beautifully printed.

Thanks also to Martin Hayden Jr. for providing photos from his father's (Martin Hayden Sr.) own 502nd Port Battalion World War II scrapbook. Dr. Marcus S. Cox, associate dean of graduate programs at Xavier University of Louisiana, for sharing his expertise in African American military history and African American history, and to Dr. Rob Citino at the National WWII Museum in New Orleans for connecting Dr. Cox with *Infinite Hope*. To Grace McKinney, Carla Carpenter, and Ella Stocker—thank you for deciphering my scrawl into typed words. A hurrah to Sarah Corson, Dick Atlee, Vanessa Robinson, and Jasmine Samuel for helping on the home front so my focus could stay on the book, and to dear Susie Valdina, for rediscovering treasures of information I'd long forgotten about. I'm also immensely grateful to the fine people at the Kislak Center of the University of Pennsylvania, who will be archiving the totality of my World War II work, making it available for generations to come. To Eva, my comrade in art, fellow Cooper Union student who studied jewelry making and metalworking, who never ever stopped writing. A hurrah-hurrah to all of my friends at Simon & Schuster, who are as excited about this book as I am. As for the Ashley Bryan Center . . . Every artist should have the support and love of such fine folks as Sandy Campbell, H. Nichols B. Clark, Verna Rae Denny, Caitlyn Dlouhy, Bari Haskins-Jackson, Dan and Cynthia Lief, Daniel Minter, Rob Snyder, and Joanne Thorman.

Finally, I am forever humbled by the courage and strength of my 502nd battalion mates, who told me time and time again: *Let us do that, Ashley, you go and draw!*

Peace and Love,

Ashley

═══ SOURCES ═══

"10 Eye-Opening Facts About World War 2." National Geographic Kids. n.d. Last accessed December 3, 2018. natgeokids.com/au/discover/history/general-history/world-war-two.

Ambrose, Stephen E. *D-Day Illustrated Edition: June 6, 1944: The Climactic Battle of World War II.* New York: Simon & Schuster, 2014.

———. *The Good Fight: How World War II Was Won.* New York: Simon & Schuster, 2001.

"An Artist at D-Day." Produced by Carol Jackson. "The Story," American Public Media, June 7, 2013. thestory.org/stories/2013-06/artist-d-day.

Ashley Bryan Center. n.d. Last accessed April 9, 2019. ashleybryancenter.org.

"Black History Month." The National WWII Museum. January 31, 2019. Last accessed February 8, 2019. nationalww2museum.org/war/articles/black-history-month.

Brozyna, Andrew J. "History of the 502nd Port Battalion." *Longshore Soldiers.* May 25, 2012. Last accessed March 7, 2019. longshoresoldiers.com/2012/05/history-of-502nd-port-battalion. html.

Delmont, Matthew. "Why African-American Soldiers Saw World War II as a Two-Front Battle." Smithsonian.com. August 24, 2017. Last accessed June 8, 2018. smithsonianmag.com/ history/why-african-american-soldiers-saw-world-war-ii-two-front-battle-180964616.

Stone, Tanya Lee. *Courage Has No Color: The True Story of the Triple Nickles America's First Black Paratroopers.* Somerville: Candlewick Press, 2013.

"World War II." DKfindout! n.d. Last accessed January 30, 2019. dkfindout.com/us/history/ world-war-ii.

To hear Ashley discuss his World War II exhibit in more detail, visit thestory.org/stories/2013-06/artist-d-day.

PHOTO & ILLUSTRATION CREDITS

Bill McGuinness: pp. 8 (stained-glass window), 9 (St. John's Evangelical Lutheran Church), 89 (stained glass and puppet)

deviantart.com/onecoldcanadian: p. 22 (crayon scribble)

Everett Collection, Inc./Alamy Stock Photo: p. 37 (propaganda movie poster)

Eye-Stock/Alamy Stock Photo: p. vi (newspaper)

FDR Presidential Library & Museum: p. 71 (Roosevelt, seated)

Flickr: p. 61 (city ruins)

Flickr/Archangel12: p. 70 (Normandy American Cemetery and Memorial)

Freepik.com: pp. vi, 14 (green paint swatch)

Henry Beer: pp. 3 (map), 48 (map)

Hulton Archives/Getty: p. 78 (soldiers on beach behind barbed wire)

iStock/milicad: p. 50 (barbed wire)

iStock/Hydromet: p. 58 (background, sand)

iStock/NadyaPhoto: pp. 62–63 (background, beach)

iStock/baona: pp. 76–77 (background, railway tracks)

Karyn Lee: title hand-lettering

Library of Congress: pp. 6 (subway platform), 21 (flag with three stars)

Martin Hayden Jr.: pp. 10–11 (military training camp), 47, 49 (background), 56 (soldiers unloading cargo), 73 (soldier with puppy), 80–81 (background)

MGPhoto76/Alamy Stock Photo: p. 78 (ruined city of Caen)

Murdo MacLeod: p. 38 (Glasgow School of Art)

National Archives: p. 28 (United We Win poster), 50–51 (soldiers on the beach), 58 (soldiers with balloons), 71 (background; Giraud, Roosevelt, de Gaulle, Churchill), 75 (atomic bomb), 77 (children eating), 81 (female soldiers)

National Park Service: p. 16 (naval yard)

Pocket Books, Inc.: p. 30 (cover image of The Pocket Book of Verse)

Shawshots/Alamy Stock Photo: jacket front panel, p. 59 (Omaha Beach)

Sherwin Grannum: p. 40 (military band)

sketchuptextureclub.com: pp. 17–18, 66 (background, cardboard)

Tim O'Brien: jacket front panel photo retouching

US Army National Archives: pp. 52–53 (background, soldiers storming the beach)

sketchuptextureclub.com: pp. 27, 76, and 97 (cardboard, background)

United States Postal Service: jacket front panel, pp. 65 (stamp), 66 (stamps), 69 (stamps)

US Army National Archives: pp. 62–63 (soldiers storming the beach)